D0575475

PARADOX AND IDENTITY IN THEOLOGY

PARADOX AND IDENTITY IN THEOLOGY

R. T. Herbert

CORNELL UNIVERSITY PRESS
ITHACA AND LONDON

First published 1979 by Cornell University Press.
Published in the United Kingdom by Cornell University Press Ltd.,
2-4 Brook Street, London W1Y 1AA.

International Standard Book Number 0-8014-1222-6
Library of Congress Catalog Card Number 78-20784
Printed in the United States of America
Librarians: Library of Congress cataloging information appears on the last page of the book.

Contents

Acknowledgments

MANY people have given me help and encouragement during the writing of this volume. I thank them all. They include Don Levi, University of Oregon; John W. Cook, Goleta, California; Dennis Holt, Southeast Missouri State College; J. William Forgie, University of California at Santa Barbara; Peter Geach, University of Leeds; Anthony Kenny, Oxford University; Terence Penelhum, University of Calgary; Peter van Inwagen, Syracuse University; Richard Creel, Ithaca College; Martin Andic, University of Massachusetts, Boston; James Edwards, Furman University; R. K. Scheer and B. R. Tilghman, Kansas State University; and the editors at Cornell University Press.

Three of the chapters of this book are revisions of journal articles. An earlier version of "Puzzle Cases and Earthquakes" appeared in *Analysis*, 28 (1967–68); "Two of Kierkegaard's Uses of 'Paradox'" appeared in *The Philosophical Review*, 70 (1961); and "The Absolute Paradox: The God-Man" was published under the title "The God-Man" in *Religious Studies*, 6 (1970).

C. S. Lewis's letter to Sister Penelope is reprinted by permission of Harcourt Brace Jovanovich, Inc., from *Letters of* C. S. *Lewis*, edited by W. H. Lewis, copyright © 1966 by W. H. Lewis and Executors of C. S. Lewis, and by permission of Curtis Brown Ltd., London, on behalf of the Estate of C. S. Lewis. Material from Vernon Pratt's *Religion and Secularization* and from D. Z. Phillips's *Death and Immortality* is reprinted by permission of St. Martin's Press, Inc., and Macmillan, London and Basingstoke.

For their patience and loving care I owe a heavy debt of gratitude to my family, to whom this book is dedicated.

R. T. HERBERT

Eugene, Oregon

PARADOX AND IDENTITY IN THEOLOGY

Oh would that there was truth in the intercourse between men! One man defends Christianity, another attacks it and in the end, if one examines their lives, neither of them bothers very much about it; perhaps it is their livelihood. . . .

—KIERKEGAARD

THOSE WINTER SUNDAYS

Sundays too my father got up early
and put his clothes on in the blueblack cold,
then with cracked hands that ached
from labor in the weekday weather made
banked fires blaze. No one ever thanked him.

I'd wake and hear the cold splintering, breaking.
When the rooms were warm, he'd call,
and slowly I would rise and dress,
fearing the chronic angers of that house,

Speaking indifferently to him,
who had driven out the cold
and polished my good shoes as well.
What did I know, what did I know
of love's austere and lonely offices?

—ROBERT HAYDEN

The Bible is not man's theology, but God's anthropology.

—A JEWISH PHILOSOPHER

Introduction

IN this book I examine certain theological doctrines which seem to be paradoxical or even contradictory: that the eternal can be found in temporal things; that we are free although God knows all we will ever think, say, or do; that though a man has died yet will he live again.

The first chapter presents a secular parable of the life of faith, launching two investigations. One of these (concluded only in Chapter 6) shows how criteria for personal identity laid down by philosophers appear to be the product of "a one-sided diet" and to constitute that illusory "law" that, as Wittgenstein says, philosophers are wont to see "in the way a word is used," a "law" whose consistent application "leads to paradoxical results" (*The Blue and Brown Books*, p. 27). Such paradoxical results are found in some philosophers' understanding of resurrection talk, and this investigation finds that those results are correctable by (among other measures) a carefully administered diet supplementing the one-sided one that produced them.

Viewed collectively and from a little distance, however, religious beliefs may not seem particularly paradoxical but instead may seem to be the products of self-deception, innocent or willful. Therefore the second investigation launched by the secular parable in Chapter 1 concerns such explanations of belief as "it's all a matter of self-willed illusion." And so before examining some theological doctrines individually, I consider in Chapter 2 a well-known example of this kind of explanation, namely, the claim made by Freud and many others that faith and doctrine itself are the products of unconscious fears and desires.

Whether such explanations succeed or fail, however, the question of paradox remains; even if belief escapes the Freudian frying pan, there is still the fire of paradox and contradiction. Thus in Chapters 3 and 4 I investigate, through an examination of Kierkegaard, the claim that paradoxes inform (infest?) faith. In Chapter 3 I examine the view that belief in God is itself paradoxical because it involves "objective uncertainty." (Cf. Freud's view in chapter 5 of *The Future of an Illusion*, that belief poses a "remarkable psychological problem" because what is believed is not "well authenticated.") In Chapter 4 I examine what is really the apex of Kierkegaard's claim that paradox informs faith: namely, the assertion that the doctrine of the incarnation is the "absolute paradox" that what is by nature eternal began to exist in time. This examination culminates in a scrutiny of perplexities in both classical and contemporary Christology that are closely related to this "paradox."

Chapter 5 turns to another paradox, the belief in God's foreknowledge and human freedom. Those who believe with C. S. Peirce that "literal foreknowledge is certainly contradictory to literal freedom" may see a paradox of the deepest kind here.

The final chapter concerns the doctrine of the general resurrection. A lengthy examination is made of the skeptical question "How can an alleged resurrectee be numerically identical with any person who has died and turned to dust?" (This question, I suspect, is the historic source of all the discussion, from Locke to the present, of the so-called problem of personal identity.)

The characteristic thrust of these chapters can be indicated by showing their position on a field where three "armies" are arrayed. The forces of philosophical skepticism (Antony Flew, Kai Nielsen, and others) are attacking; the army of philosophical theism (P. T. Geach, Anthony Kenny, and others) defends; the army of so-called fideism (D. Z. Phillips, Rush Rhees, and others) also defends. The battle is over religious doctrines. Skepticism seeks to destroy them by showing them to be unintelligible or confused. Theism defends them by attempting to show that skepticism's demonstrations fail. Geach describes theism's strategy clearly when he writes: "What I am maintaining is that for each single argument against faith there is a refutation, in terms of ordinary logic; not that there is some one general technique for refuting all arguments against faith, or even all arguments against a particular dogma of faith."[1] Fideism also defends against skepticism but does so by ignoring or abandoning what skepticism is attacking and taking up a position out of range of its demonstrations. Fideism undertakes this maneuver convinced that those demonstrations have succeeded: that religious doctrines, at least as skepticism and theism conceive them, are shown to be unintelligible. Fideism's own conception of religious doctrines or beliefs can perhaps best be intimated by citing what a leading fideist, D. Z. Phillips, says concerning one of them: "Eternity is not an extension of this present life, but a mode of judging it. . . . Questions about the immortality of the soul are seen not to be questions concerning the extent of a man's life, and in particular concerning whether that life can extend beyond the grave, but questions concerning the kind of life a man is living."[2] Skepticism and theism would both disagree with this. They would insist that such questions do concern a life beyond the grave (as well, perhaps, as the kind of life a man is now living). Generally, it seems that fideism conceives the religious doctrines to have only a psychological or anthropological and nonsupernatural import, whereas both theism and skepticism, while disagreeing over whether the doctrines are after all intelligible, conceive them to have, essentially, a supernatural or metaphysical intention.

The present volume joins the ranks of theism and employs

wherever possible the strategy suggested by Geach in the remark quoted above (this strategy's most sustained employment is found in Chapter 6).

Another point needs to be stressed. It concerns the character of the issues discussed in this book and the consequent character of the theism embraced. The issues are philosophical ones. Roughly speaking they concern questions of intelligibility rather than truth. Thus the theism espoused supposes, and seeks to exhaust skepticism's opposition to, merely the intelligibility of certain religious doctrines. Such an enterprise may seem modest, but if successfully carried out it yields a result that even the unbeliever will have to accept: namely, that there is no good reason to deny or doubt the intelligibility or coherence of, for example, the doctrine of the general resurrection or that of the incarnation.

The martial figure of speech I have been employing here may be slightly misleading in creating the impression that the doctrines being attacked and defended are each and every one of them most worthy of defense. This, I think, cannot safely be assumed, for since theologians normally play an important role in their formulation, some of the doctrines may really be infested by incoherence. If philosophy is still sometimes theology's handmaid, she must also sometimes be theology's schoolmistress, rapping her pupil's knuckles for slovenly ratiocinative deportment. Perhaps, then, our martial figure of speech should give place to a legal one, which not only avoids the false suggestion of its predecessor but indicates more definitely the spirit in which these six chapters are offered.

Each chapter starts from the presumption that the religious and theological language and doctrines examined are innocent of incoherence and unintelligibility until proven guilty. But of course anything to which this principle is applied is already in the dock and would not be there unless suspected and indicted. These chapters, then, are trials; they prosecute and they defend.

Sometimes, as in Chapter 6, the defendant is found not guilty; at other times, as in Chapter 5, a defendant (the orthodox account of divine foreknowledge) is found guilty, or at least strong reasons for so finding are adduced. But every verdict is subject to appeal. Therefore, if it please the reader, he may review these proceedings to determine whether there has been any miscarriage of justice.

1 / Puzzle Cases and Earthquakes

I

ON the morning of February 17, 1956, the man known as Erik, chauffeur to the famous Finnish conductor Eino Viljanen, awoke in his room in Viljanen's New York household. He opened his eyes, looked sleepily around the room for a moment, then muttered, "What am I doing here?" Trying to remember, he placed his hand on the back of his neck. The skin felt coarse and his neck strangely large. He thought, "What's wrong with me?" and looked at his hand. "What's wrong with my hand? It's swollen." He peered at it and was about to touch it with his other hand to see if it would pain him when he noticed that his other hand, too, was swollen. "What's happened to me!" he cried in fright and leaped up to look at himself in the mirror. Glancing in the mirror, he shouted, "Erik, you fool, get out of the way so I can see myself!" And then he thought, confused, "My voice. It sounds so strange!" and, "But if I see Erik's reflection in the mirror, how can I be seeing the mirror at all? He should be between me and it." He leaned forward and peered closely at his reflection, touched his face in several places with the tips of his fingers, noticed the reflection of his hand move and then touched the mirror. "How can this be?" he thought. "Can *I* be Erik? No, no, I'm *Eino*—Eino Viljanen!" He whirled and left the room to find Volter Viljanen, the conductor's son.

Volter was in the large sitting room and looked up sadly when the figure of Erik burst into the room. "Volter, Volter, tell me who I am! Am I Erik or am I Eino Viljanen, your father?"

"Erik, please. Father's death has been too much for you. Sit down," said Volter kindly.

"Erik? He addresses me as Erik and says that I am dead," thought "Erik,"[1] "but he doesn't recognize me because something has happened to my body so that it looks like Erik's." And aloud to Volter he said, "If you think I am Erik, call for Erik to come in. See us standing side by side. Then you will know I am your father." And he added to himself, "How strange, too, is my voice! It is *like* Erik's. Deep. Yet Erik's. . . ."

"How strange," thought Volter, "is Erik's voice. It is, as always, deep. But his words are clear and crisp and come out at a great rate and with a fast tremolo, very much in the way Father's did." Then looking curiously at the man before him, he said, "Come into the next room. Father's, Eino Viljanen's, body is lying in state. You must be made to realize that he is dead. He died yesterday. You yourself carried his body in from the garden, where he had fallen dead of a heart attack." They stood before the coffin and looked down at the body of Viljanen.

Bewildered and shaken, "Erik" said, "Volter, I do not know what has happened; that is my body and this is Erik's." He was silent. "Listen to me. Can Erik play the piano, the cello? Does he know music? No. But *I* can play the piano and the cello. *I* can conduct an orchestra. I know many scores by heart. Listen." And he went to the piano and played, while Volter sat and listened in amazement to his father's favorite pieces and he saw that they were being played as his father had played them, except for suggestions of awkwardness in passages difficult to finger—at which points the player cursed the "sausages" he now had for fingers.

To continue in more summary fashion: in the days and weeks that followed it was seen that "Erik" could "remember" the past of Viljanen in as much detail and as readily as the old man himself had, and his feats of "memory" and memorization were as astounding. His musicianship, at least as a conductor ("Erik" was allowed and even urged by certain people—the question of their motives aside for the present—to "resume" Viljanen's musical career), his artistic integrity, and the quality of his orchestra's performances were, even to the most discriminating critics, indistinguishable from Viljanen's own; even his rages and tantrums over what he considered imperfect performances matched Viljanen's, both in intensity and kind (for instance, like Viljanen, "Erik" ordinarily snatched up his extra batons and broke them in his hands, upset every inanimate object he could, and tore his collar to shreds). He could, like Viljanen, exhibit devilish cunning in abusing a player who had made a mistake; and, like Viljanen, he enjoyed fast car rides, Broadway musicals, practical jokes and TV boxing matches, was given to childish self-pity and rudeness, ordinarily ate sparingly and slept little, and had a remarkable power over everyone associated with him. Whether grave, gay, vengeful or beneficent, he magnetized his players, his servants, his friends and even his family. They wilted under his frown and basked in his smile. They rushed to fulfill his every wish, looking upon it as a favor conferred by him.

II

Consider now the following argument made by B. A. O. Williams:

> Suppose a person A to undergo a sudden change, and to acquire a character exactly like that of some person known to have lived in

> the past, B. Suppose him further to make sincere memory claims which entirely fit the life of B. We might think these conditions sufficient for us to identify A (as he now is) with B. But they are not. For another contemporary person, C, might undergo an exactly similar change at the same time as A, and if the conditions were sufficient to say that A = B, they would be sufficient to say that C = B as well. But it cannot be the case both that A = B and C = B, for, were it so, it would follow that A = C, which is absurd. One can avoid this absurdity by abandoning one or both of the assertions A = B and C = B. But it would be vacuous to assert one of these and abandon the other, since there is nothing to choose between them; hence, the rational course is to abandon both. Therefore . . . it would be just as vacuous to make the identification with B even if only one contemporary were involved.[2]

I shall now apply this argument to our case of Viljanen and Erik. Since we can imagine that Erik has undergone the changes we have described—that is, that he now has talents, habits, mannerisms, and so forth, exactly like those Viljanen had and that he now makes sincere memory claims all of which fit Viljanen's past—we may think that these conditions warrant our saying that Erik is now Viljanen. They do not, however. For if we can imagine these changes in Erik, we can imagine them also to occur at the same time in someone else, for instance, Basil the gardener. And if this change in Erik warrants our saying that he is Viljanen, then the same change in Basil warrants our saying that he, too, is Viljanen. But it cannot be that both Erik and Basil are Viljanen, "for were it so, it would follow that [Erik is Basil], which is absurd." (According to Williams's original version of the argument, contained in "Personal Identity and Individuation,"[3] what would be said to follow and to be absurd is that Viljanen "would be in two places at once.") To avoid this absurdity one can abandon the assertion that Basil is Viljanen, or else one can abandon the assertion that Erik is Viljanen. But to abandon one of these assertions rather than the other would be vacuous, "since there is nothing to choose between them; hence the rational course is to abandon both." If, then, it is vacuous to say either that Erik is Viljanen or that Basil is Viljanen in the situation involving Basil, it is vacuous to say that Erik is Viljanen in the situation not involving Basil. We may add here, in accordance with the original version of Williams's argument, that the most one can say, in the situation not involving Basil, is that Erik's personality is now exactly like Viljanen's and that his memory claims fit Viljanen's past life.

This argument clearly shows the absurdity of thinking that, as Williams puts it, there are "grounds to justify a judgement of identity as against a judgement of exact similarity" in the Viljanen case. But although his argument admirably accomplishes this end, there is something misleading in it. I shall try to make clear what I mean.

To do this, we shall return to a consideration of the detail of the Viljanen case. "Erik" has awakened, looked at himself in the mirror, burst in upon Volter, crying out, "Volter, what has happened to me?" Volter takes "Erik" to be upset over Viljanen's death, but notices that "Erik's" voice has become like Viljanen's. They walk to the coffin and look at Viljanen's body. "Erik" is thunderstruck. Then, his composure to a degree returned, he goes to the piano and plays, while Volter sits amazed to hear his father's favorite pieces played as his father had played them.

Imagine then the following scene: "Erik" finished playing and, somewhat calmed, rose from the bench and, smiling at Volter (the smile, Volter noticed, was delicate, with the lips closed, like his father's, a smile that startled him, for he had not supposed "Erik's" features capable of it), said, "Now, my son, what do you say?"

Ashen, Volter rose, stared for a moment at the face, blinked his stinging eyes, and tried to speak. "I—I, please. I must think."

"Yes," said "Erik"; "how strange all this is. For it isn't, as I had first thought, as though something terrible had happened to my body—as though it had suddenly grown. It's that I no longer have the *same* body at all! Am I then no longer myself? I must confess that when I was going toward the piano to play, I thought, 'And what if I *can't* play?' The idea dizzied me. But I am all right now. Oh, of course, with these fingers I am clumsy and I. . . ." He broke off and gazed at Volter. "Yes, I can see you are in a whirl. I don't blame you. Sit down again, and listen while I try the cello."

Volter sat down abruptly as "Erik" turned to the instrument. He sat tense and haggard with eyes glistening and hands tightly clasped before him while "Erik" expertly tuned his cello.

Then "Erik" played. The somber sounds filled the room, and in them Volter again heard his father's playing. After a time, Volter got up from his chair and walked, haltingly, with head bowed, to the side of the player. For a moment he stood listening, or as though listening; then he touched "Erik's" shoulder lightly with his hand. The player stopped and stood up, looking into Volter's eyes.

Now, what can be imagined to have happened next? Is not the following imaginable? Volter looked for a moment into the eyes that were gazing into his own. Then there came from him in a kind of sob the words "*My father!*" The other sighed and murmured, "Yes, my son. And do you know—I was terribly afraid in these last few moments that I would be—alone."

If it is possible to imagine this reaction in Volter, then it is also possible to imagine his "living it out," to imagine that his attitude and relation to "Erik" are what they were to Viljanen, that the whole remainder of his life is, as it were, played in the new key announced by the words "my father." And if it is possible to imagine this reaction and new life in Volter's case, then surely it is also possible to do the same concerning other intimates of Viljanen. They call him Viljanen, and their thoughts and feelings, as well as their behavior, accord with this practice. If they meet him on the street, they greet him with "Hello, Eino"; if he reminisces at the dinner table about "his" boyhood in Helsinki, they enjoy the anecdote and marvel at his powers of recollection and do not think "But, after all, it is not *his* boyhood he is talking about. He isn't really *recollecting* anything." Such thoughts never occur to them. And if some outsider at table should rudely give voice to these or like thoughts, they would lower their eyes in embarrassment or be angry.

We are now in a position to state what is misleading about Williams's argument: the argument is misleading in that it implies that everyone who is not forgetting what the argument is calculated to remind him of will in fact make the same judgment about, say, the Viljanen case—everyone, that is to say, including those who, like Volter, are intimately involved. Thus, anyone who is not forgetting will judge only that Erik is exactly like Viljanen and never that Erik *is* Viljanen. For such a person realizes that since Erik's body and Viljanen's body are not the same one, a "ground" necessary to judging that Erik is Viljanen is absent.

If then, Williams's argument were correct in this implication, it would have to be supposed that Volter is somehow forgetting, perhaps in the excitement of the wonderful situation in which he finds himself, what the argument is calculated to remind him of.

We shall imagine Volter to speak for himself in discussion with Williams here:

Volter: "No; I am not forgetting that anyone making truthful utterances of the forms 'So and so is Mr. X,' 'That is Mr. X,' 'This is my uncle,' and so forth, knows or supposes, to put it roughly and briefly, that only one body is in the relevant way involved. Nor am I forgetting that more than one body is involved in this case. But even though I am not forgetting these things, still I say that this is my father."

Williams: "But how can you say that he is your father! What is *meant* by this? Must it not mean only that he is exactly like your father, or, if you wish, *amazingly* like your father? For if you really do have in mind what my argument is intended to remind you of, you *must* see that the grounds you have justify your saying only that he is amazingly like your father. And if you insist on saying that he *is* your father, then this can only be understood to mean that he is amazingly like him."[4]

Volter: "Does not saying that he is amazingly like my father involve having a certain attitude? If I, for example, said this, involved would be this, that I should feel uneasy in his presence, and when he called me 'son' I should want to ask him not to do so. Also, when I heard his playing, I should, I suppose, be struck by its *uncanny resemblance* to my father's. In general, I should regard him as nothing so much as a curiosity—and all the warmth and love I feel for him would be gone.

"You see, then, why I do not say that he is amazingly like my father. For with this expression goes an attitude that I just do not have. On the other hand, the attitude I do have toward this man is well expressed in my answering you with 'He is my father,' and also in my continuing to use, in other contexts, the words 'my father' in referring to him. When he reminisces about the time ten years ago when he took me to the beach and taught me to swim, *I do not think*, 'But it wasn't he who took me. He doesn't really *remember* this.'[5] My attitude toward him is my attitude toward my father, and his attitude toward me is the attitude of my father toward me. I *could* not declare that he is amazingly like my father. Nor could I allow that when I say that he is my father, this can mean only that he is amazingly like him.

"If you are astounded (as you no doubt are) at what I have been saying, if you find it incredible, for instance, that when I listen to him talk about the day at the beach, I simply do not think things like 'But *you* are not the one who took me there,' but instead look into his face alight with the reminiscence of a pleasant time and perhaps say, 'Oh, yes! We had fun!'—then I can say only that you should come and stay with us for a while. Get to know our lives first hand, and give yourself the opportunity of being impressed by the serene and perfect assurance of the man in every moment of his existence. Then perhaps—just perhaps—your present attitude will melt away."

Thus far concerning Williams's argument, we have said the following. The argument is calculated to remind its reader that in judgments of identity of persons only one body is involved. There is in the argument the implication that anyone who is not forgetting this reminder will in fact not make such a judgment in cases in which he knows or assumes more than one body to be involved. But we have seen how things stand with Volter. He says that he is not forgetting the reminder of Williams's argument. And yet despite this, he says such things as "I would like you to meet my father," "Viljanen is over there by the library table," "My father is at rehearsal," "He is my father," and "Oh, yes, there's my father."

But here a defender of Williams's position speaks: "Even if Volter does *say* such things, he is not making true judgments of identity. If he is to do that, his utterances must have the *same meaning* in the 'Erik' period as they would have had in the pre-'Erik' period. For example, 'Oh, yes, there's my father over there,' spoken at a crowded party to signal discovery, must have the same meaning whether spoken before or spoken after Erik became 'Erik.' But the utterance cannot have the same meaning in the 'Erik' period as before. For the grounds for the use of the phrase 'my father' here, grounds present before the change, no longer remain. It is no longer the case that only one body is in the relevant way involved. Thus despite the fact that Volter's post-change utterances are apparently judgments of identity, and despite the fact that Volter takes them to be such judgments, they cannot be true judgments of identity. For the grounds necessary for them to have the *meaning* of such judgments are now absent."

Volter need not, however, accede to the claim that is central to this argument. He need not agree that because the grounds mentioned are no longer present, the meaning of his utterances can no longer be the same as before. He can insist that despite the absence of those grounds, the meaning is the same *because the role or roles the utterances play are the same as before.* He can observe that even his post-change use of "There is my father next to the piano" would have its usual contrast with "Oh, that's not my father, but it certainly looks like him."

In making this reply Volter would be meeting one thesis about sameness of the meaning of his personal-identity judgments with a thesis of his own. To the thesis that the meaning of his utterances remains the same after the change only if the (one-body) grounds are still present, he opposes his own thesis that their meaning remains the same if their role or roles remain the same.

It seems, then, that one may affirm or one may deny that Volter's judgments of identity are true ones and that one's stand on this matter will depend on which one of the above theses he adopts or is inclined to adopt.

And how one is inclined on this point will depend, I think, on his reaction *in* the situation. One *might* react as we have imagined Volter to do, in which case one will be inclined to identify meaning here with role; or one might *not* react as Volter reacts, in which case one will be inclined to say that meaning is here determined by the "one-body" grounds.

How one would *in fact* react in such a case would depend largely upon one's situation in the case. If one is an intimate, as Volter is in the case we have imagined, the chances are much greater that one will react as Volter does. If, on the other hand, one is remote from the details and has no close human ties with the principal, the chances are greater that one will react as Williams evidently thinks every reasonable man would. But of course one's situation in the case would not be the sole determinant of one's reaction. It is not difficult, for instance, to imagine Volter reacting in a way quite different from the way we have imagined. He might, after all, have approached "Erik" at that crucial moment only to reject him. It is, I think, partly because of the particular case Williams chooses to work with that he finds it unquestionable that everyone who has his argument or reminder in mind will say the same thing about such puzzle cases. The case is one in which Charles, a contemporary of ours, is imagined to undergo changes that make him exactly like Guy Fawkes, whose dates are 1570–1606. Since we are all equally remote from Guy Fawkes, we cannot imagine ourselves to be struck by Charles's new behavior as being that of that gentleman. Of *this* case, then, we *would* all very likely say the same thing.

If, now, what we have been saying is correct, we have seen that the implication of Williams's argument is quite misleading: a person may very well have firmly in mind Williams's reminder that judgments of identity have as their ground the fact that only one body is in the relevant way involved and, despite having this fact in mind, make judgments of identity—and in this person's life, in *his* circle, they would *be* judgments of identity; for they would have the same role or roles in his life as judgments of identity have in the lives of those in ordinary circumstances. Nothing in Williams's argument seems to disallow this.

III

Several points emerge from, or are suggested by, the foregoing pages. I will introduce the first point by adapting some sentences from G. C. Nerlich's "'Continuity' Continued."[6] "The central question is what [Volter] takes himself to *mean* when he asserts identity in [the Viljanen case] . . . the challenge is to produce the set of sufficient conditions which yields identity, but leaves [bodily] continuity out. . . . If when [Volter] asserts identity in [the Viljanen case], he does mean to assert more than exact similarity, then *what* more does he mean to assert? And which feature realized in [the case] supports this more, whatever it is?

What, after all, are the conditions being appealed to as sufficient?"

These sentences make it clear that, like Williams, Nerlich supposes that "grounds" or "conditions" determine meaning here. He is saying that since there is no feature in the case which supports, no set of sufficient conditions which yields, identity, Volter cannot *mean* identity when he asserts it; that at best he can mean only similarity; for that is all that the features realized support, all that the conditions are sufficient to yield.

It is because Nerlich supposes that "grounds" or "conditions" determine meaning in our (or any) case that he views his challenge "to produce the set of sufficient conditions which yields identity, but leaves [bodily] continuity out" as unanswerable. But so far from being unanswerable, it simply is no challenge at all to Volter and his circle, who do not make Nerlich's assumption about meaning in our case. To one who in some particular case does not assume that meaning is determined by grounds or sufficient conditions, but instead thinks that it is to be accounted for in some other way, producing a set of sufficient conditions which yields identity will be unnecessary and the challenge to do so irrelevant. Thus, Volter says that in this case he identifies meaning with role or use, that in his circle judgments of identity with regard to "Erik" have the *meaning* of judgments of identity in that they have the same uses or roles in his circle as judgments of identity do in the lives of people in ordinary circumstances. And Volter might issue a challenge of his own: if you do not think that we *mean* identity when we assert it, come and see what we *do* with those assertions, how they are woven into our days. To repeat, Volter supposes that the meaning of these assertions resides just in the pattern of that weave; thus for the case of "Erik" Volter rejects Williams's and Nerlich's supposition concerning the meaning of judgments of personal identity and replaces it with a supposition of his own. It should be emphasized, moreover, that this does not show, nor does it commit Volter to the belief, that their supposition has no *general* validity, that is, no application to normal, nonpuzzle, cases. Rather, it is (at least) a reminder that in doing philosophy here, as elsewhere, one ought to put down the temptation to (in Wittgenstein's phrase) "see a law in the way a word is used" (*The Blue and Brown Books*, p. 27).

I now turn to the second point. We see that Nerlich's position suggests that he would ask Volter what he takes himself to mean when he asserts identity in the Viljanen case. And we see that to Nerlich this would amount to a demand to be shown "sufficient conditions" which obviously are not present. But to someone else the question as to what Volter and his circle mean might be something quite different. If in imagination one looks at the lives of Volter and his circle, sees in detail how they live, comes to "know" them as intimately as they know one another, one's imagined reaction might be: "But I do not understand these people. I too address 'Erik' as Viljanen and refer to him as Viljanen, but I do this only because they do who are my friends. I do not really *mean* it, whereas they obviously do. They do not intend to deceive one another, but at times I can but feel that they are a community of the self-deceived, that their whole way of life with regard to 'Viljanen' is a monstrous, solemn charade by which they themselves are taken in. And yet of course it is not a charade of any sort. The thing is eerie.—At any rate, *I* do not understand them, I cannot participate."

That our speaker does not understand means roughly that he cannot participate in a form of life,[7] not (as with Nerlich) that he notices the absence of certain conditions whose presence (he supposes) is required. Our speaker's position with regard to Volter's circle is rather like that of Steiner, the double filicide and suicide in the Fellini film *La Dolce Vita*, with regard to Christianity. Steiner hovers around the edges of Christianity, looking wistfully toward its center. He discusses its concepts knowledgeably with his friends, some of whom are churchmen. He regularly goes to a cathedral to play Bach joyously on its great organ. But, as a friend of mine has pointed out to me, Steiner cannot pray. And this epitomizes the fact that he cannot participate in the form of life that Christianity is. He can, no doubt, *recite* the prayers of the church, but he cannot pray them; just as our speaker can address "Erik" as Viljanen and refer to him as Viljanen, but cannot (in Nerlich's language) "mean identity." For, like praying, meaning identity here is essentially bound up with participating in a certain form of life. And though both Steiner and our speaker in one sense understand a form of life, they cannot participate in it, and in *this* sense do *not* understand the participants and what they say.

Nerlich asks what feature realized in our case supports the identity that Volter means to assert. *No* feature realized in the case supports this. (Much less does Volter's asserting it *with great feeling* support it, supposing he did on occasion so assert it.) There is only the fact that Volter and his circle participate in a form of life. And this fact does not support, does not constitute a set of sufficient conditions that yields, the identity that they mean to assert. Saying that it does would be tantamount to saying that we all *must* agree, not in opinion, but in form of life (see Wittgenstein's *Philosophical Investigations*, sec. 241). But of course there can be no necessity here. "What has to be accepted, the given, is—so one could say—*forms of life*" (*Philosophical Investigations*, p. 226). Applied to our case, this remark of course does not mean that we would all have to accept, to become participants in, Volter's form of life. It means that as *philosophers* we must see the form of life as a "protophenomenon" and say, "*This language-game is played.*"

The foregoing shows that two sorts of understanding are conceivable with regard to the Viljanen case.[8] The one is philosophical or intellectual, and its absence stems from being guided by a restricting presupposition about meaning. Nerlich and Williams are, I think, so guided. The other sort of understanding I will call spiritual, and its absence (or presence), at least with respect to our puzzle case, is perhaps impossible to explain. What makes Volter, standing before the figure of "Erik," sob out the words "My father"? What accounts for this earthquake and the form of life to which it gives rise?

But instead of saying that an explanation in this case is perhaps impossible, I should have said that for those in Volter's circle no explanation would be acceptable, whereas for those outside his circle some explanation might be. This can be made clear by considering again the case of Steiner. Why can Steiner not participate? Why can he not pray? To those within the circle of Christianity, the satisfactory explanation is that Steiner—who, though an atheist, is, it must be remembered, seeking—lacks God's grace.[9] To them, Steiner lacks the light-giving, heart-changing, man-changing gift which they themselves, without meriting it, have received. To those outside the circle of Christianity, on the other hand, saying that the wistful outsider lacks God's grace or that those within the circle have been given that grace, cannot serve as the satisfactory explanation, for, of course, those outside the circle do not believe in the gift or the Giver. Instead, their explanation, if they have one, will probably contain allusions to Freud or to flat dottiness.

Likewise, with respect to the Viljanen case, the outsider's explanation (of, for example, Volter's reaction and subsequent life) will probably be Freudian. But of course no insider (such as Volter) could accept such an explanation, for this would amount to his accepting as true something like this: "'Erik' is not really Viljanen, Volter's father; Volter merely wishes (unconsciously) that he were and as a consequence 'adopts' him as a sort of foster-father." And his accepting this as true would be tantamount to his falling from his circle, his form of life. And why should he accept this explanation? Only people who are troubled submit themselves to psychoanalysis, and Volter is not troubled.

But unlike the Christian, who can explain Steiner to himself and to fellow Christians, Volter has no explanation with which to counter the outsider's Freudian one. For in the Viljanen case there are no concepts analogous to the concepts of a gift of grace and of a Giver of that grace. That is to say, there are no concepts which (a) can be employed to explain why the wistful outsider (like our speaker above) cannot participate and also (b) in their employment do not represent participants in a way that they cannot accept while remaining participants.

But just as above we asked: Why should Volter accept a Freudian explanation? so here we can ask: Why should he have an explanation to counter it, such as the Christian has? Why should its absence be an embarrassment? For surely he can say (speaking of the earthquake), "I suddenly knew in my very heart that it was my father. What made me (and my circle) certain I cannot say. Nor can I say why others, equally close to him, are equally certain that he is not my father and instead only out of courtesy to us call him Viljanen." That Volter can say no more than this, that no move comparable to that open to the Christian is open to him, does not leave him and his circle less immune to the outsider's explanation than the Christian is. For just as in the Christian case the move involving "gift" and "Giver" cannot be acceptable to the outsider regardless of whether he has a counterexplanation, so in the Viljanen case the Freudian explanation cannot be acceptable to the insider regardless of whether *he* has a counterexplanation.

Finally, it remains to discuss one aspect of the relationship between philosophical or intellectual understanding and spirtual understanding—in other words, between being able to give, for philosophical purposes, an accurate description of a form of life and the language involved in it, and being able to participate in that form of life. Is being able to participate necessary to being able to give an accurate description? I think that the answer to this question is "No, but. . . ."

One can give an accurate description of, say, the form of life of

Volter's circle including the language it employs without oneself being able to participate. Analogously, though this is an extrapolation from the character of Steiner presented in the film, it would not greatly surprise us to learn that Steiner has written a book, praised by believers and unbelievers alike, accurately depicting Christian life and Christian concepts. Yet Steiner himself cannot participate; he is the wistful atheist.

And yet though we might not be *greatly* surprised to learn that Steiner has written such a book, perhaps we would be *somewhat* surpised. That is to say, though being able to participate in a form of life would not be *necessary* to being able to give an accurate description, inability to participate might well raise in many a formidable barrier to generating the passion and objectivity needed to achieve the telling, truth-telling phrase—thus making it temptingly easy unintentionally to give a subtly, though perhaps deeply, distorted account. Surely this happens in the philosophy of religion. And so one might suspect that it happens also in the area of the puzzle case. But whether it does cannot, I suppose, be known. For who can tell whether, if he were confronted by the situation faced by Volter, he would be visited by an earthquake?

2 / Paradox—or Illusion?

I

IN a book entitled *Religion and Secularization*, Vernon Pratt deftly sketches a change that has taken place in our "intellectual climate." It is a transformation that came about in the scant fifty-year period between the career of Henry Sidgwick, the nineteenth-century English moral philosopher, and that of the economist John Maynard Keynes. Pratt indicates its nature by quoting a remark made by Keynes about Sidgwick. Keynes wonders how a man of Sidgwick's intelligence and sensitivity could have spent so much time and energy worrying about whether a certain doctrine is true when he knew all along that it is false. The doctrine in question is Christianity, and Keynes's puzzled words are these: "Have you ever read Sidgwick's Life? Very interesting and depressing. He never did anything but wonder whether Christianity was true, and prove that it wasn't, and hope that it was. . . . He really ought to have got over that a little sooner, because he knew that the thing wasn't true perfectly well from the beginning." Pratt goes on to comment: "About half a century separates these two men; and in that time the 'intellectual climate,' if that is the appropriate phrase, has altered, to the extent that of two equally intelligent, sensitive people one can find it necessary to devote immense intellectual and emotional energy to the question of Christianity's truth, while another finds it *obviously* false."

There you have the change. Eighty years ago enlightened people worried about the question of the truth of Christianity, seriously debated the question of God's existence. Now, however, their contemporary counterparts, it is Pratt's view, take it for granted that, in Norman Kemp Smith's words, "belief in God is no longer possible for any really enlightened mind."

It is possible, I suppose, to question whether the alleged alteration in our intellectual climate has in fact taken place. Are we living in an altered, a secularized intellectual climate? Well, the archbishops and bishops of the Anglican Church evidently think so. Pratt tells us that at a recent Lambeth Conference they wrote: "We . . . are aware of the extent to which the very thought of God seems to be passing away from the minds and hearts of many even in nominally Christian nations."

For the purposes of this discussion, I am going to assume[1] that the archbishops and bishops and Vernon Pratt and of course many others who maintain the same view are right about the matter. What I wish to concern myself with is what might reasonably be counted one of the causes of this change. What I have in mind is Freudian theory, and, specifically, Freudian theory as Freud himself applied it to religious beliefs. I will not, however, be asking whether his theory *is* a cause of the change described. I want, for my purposes here, to grant that it is—to agree with those who say that Freudian theory, along with modern astronomy and evolutionary theory, has caused basic reversals in Western man's conception of himself and of his world, has brought about fundamental alterations in his intellectual life and in his very reactions. Consider, as an illustration of a Freudian influence on our reactions, how a good many people would react at a party to an innocent young woman's recital of a dream in which she is pursued by an old man in a stovepipe hat; she manages to escape him because his hat keeps falling off, so that he has to keep stopping to retrieve it and put it on again. Some people would, of course, smile knowingly at this. Why wouldn't their grandfathers eighty years ago have done so? Because Freud's work on dreams had not yet been published to find its way into our cultural-intellectual bloodstream. Our grandfathers would have reacted to the dream with simple interest in an amusing and mildly suspenseful episode and to the young woman herself in a quite uncomplicated way. We, on the other hand, thanks to Freud, are apt to see both the dream and the dreamer quite differently. Our reaction to the dream will perhaps be one of knowing amusement at a covert and unintentional bit of bawdry. And we will perhaps regard the young woman as wonderfully and even *suspiciously* naive about a distinctly unladylike ingredient of her own mind. We react differently, and what largely accounts for the difference is Freud.

Similarly, a sensitive intellectual today may have a different reaction to Christianity from that of his nineteenth-century counterpart. He may find Christianity obviously false, whereas his counterpart was apt to find it true, or at least not clearly false. We saw this to be so in the case of Keynes and Sidgwick.

And there is another similarity between the dream case and the case of Christianity. Just as we might be tempted to regard the young woman as wonderfully and even suspiciously naive, as feeling something she won't admit, even to herself, that she feels, as after all deceiving herself—so also one like Keynes, to whom Christianity is obviously false may see any intellectually sensitive religious believer or even any fence-sitter, like Sidgwick, as suspiciously naive, as indeed deceiving himself. This is in fact how Keynes did regard Sidgwick. He says that Sidgwick "really ought to have got over [his religious doubts] a little sooner, because he knew that [Christianity] wasn't true perfectly well from the beginning."

Now the view of the believer as self-deceiver, like the similar view of the dreamer, is a Freudian sort of view. The remark about Sidgwick, like the knowing smiles over the dream, is a symptom of the presence of something Freudian in our cultural bloodstream. This is not a thesis I wish to argue for, as I said before. I leave that to the cultural anthropologist and the historian of ideas. What I will do instead is to take it for granted that the Freudian something is in our cultural bloodstream and then go on to ask whether we ought to be happy about its presence there. More specifically, I will examine two of Freud's theses concerning religion with a view to determining their acceptability at an intellectual level. And if we find that they are not acceptable, then, if in fact they are in our cultural bloodstream, our finding them unacceptable is the natural first step toward neutralizing them and their effects.

II

These two theses are set forth in Freud's little book, *The Future of an Illusion*. One concerns the origin of Judaeo-Christianity. The other concerns the individual believer's acceptance of its doctrines. I will not in what follows make any special point of distinguishing Judaism from Christianity. Freud did not find it necessary to do so for his purposes, nor do I for mine.

According to Freud, the "religious ideas" that constitute the religion are "created, born from man's need to make his helplessness tolerable" (*FI*, p. 25).* The helplessness Freud means is helplessness in the face of danger from two sources. One source is nature herself. "There are the elements, which seem to mock at all human control: the earth, which quakes and is torn apart and buries all human life and its works; water, which deluges and

*Throughout this chapter all page references to *The Future of an Illusion* will be to the Doubleday paperback edition (1964) and will be abbreviated to *FI*, followed by the page number.

drowns everything in a turmoil; storms, which blow everything before them; there are diseases, which we have only recently recognized as attacks by other organisms; and finally there is the painful riddle of death against which no medicine has yet been found, nor probably will be. With these forces," says Freud, "nature rises up against us, majestic, cruel and inexorable" (*FI*, pp. 20–21).

The other source of danger confronting which we feel our helplessness is human society, civilization. The evils and defects of civilization, the sufferings people inflict on one another through wars and other forms of inhumanity, impress on us again the fact of our own weakness (*FI*, p. 21). Thus, twin dangers—nature's cruelty and civilization's evils—make us realize our helplessness in the world, and from the need to make this helplessness tolerable Judaeo-Christianity is created.

How, according to Freud, does this religion fulfill the function of making our helplessness tolerable? By teaching that "everything that happens in this world is an expression of the intentions of an intelligence superior to us, which in the end, though its ways and byways are difficult to follow, orders everything for the best—that is, to make it enjoyable for us . . . [that] in the end all good is rewarded and all evil punished, if not actually in this form of life then in the later existences that begin after death. In this way all the terrors, the sufferings and hardships of life are destined to be obliterated. Life after death . . . brings us all the perfection that we may perhaps have missed here" (*FI*, pp. 26–27). Our helplessness is made tolerable by the religious "ideas" or doctrines that whatever adversity befalls us is ultimately for our good and that God will reward good, if not in this life, then in the next, with all perfections.

But how could a need to make our helplessness tolerable create, give birth to the body of beliefs that are the center of the Judaeo-Christian religion? Freud's answer to this question is complex. Only part of it is important for our purposes, however, that having to do with the genesis of gods (who, says Freud, later become "condensed" into the God of the Old and New Testaments). Wishing, Freud says, plays a part in the genesis of gods, as it also does in dream-life. Here is his elaboration of this claim.

> The sleeper may be seized with a presentiment of death, which threatens to place him in the grave. But the dream-work knows how to select a condition that will turn even that dreaded event into a wish-fulfilment; the dreamer sees himself in an ancient Etruscan grave which he has climbed down into, happy to find his archaeological interests satisfied. In the same way, a man makes the forces of nature not simply into persons with whom he can associate as he would with his equals—that would not do justice to the overpowering impression which those forces make on him—but he gives them the character of a father. He turns them into gods. (*FI*, pp. 23–24]

Thus Freud explains a crucial first step in the genesis of Judaeo-Christianity by drawing an analogy with his explanation of the genesis of dreams. As a sleeper may be seized with a presentiment of death, so human beings are terrified by the forces of nature. The dreaded event of death may, through such processes as displacement and symbolization, be turned into a dream that is a wish-fulfillment: for example, a dream in which the dreamer happily finds his archaeological interests satisfied. The terrifying forces of nature are, "in the same way," turned into gods that are a wish-fulfillment: gods who "exorcize the terrors of nature" (*FI*, p. 24).

Roughly put, Freud's thesis about the origin of Judaeo-Christianity—or, at least, of the *core* of it—is this. People find themselves in a fearful, indifferent world where life is nasty, brutish, and short. Longing to live in a world that is filled with love, they invent—or something in them invents—an illusion that satisfies that longing, a "dream" that fulfills that wish.

This account, like every other such naturalistic account of the origin of Christianity,[2] would of course be vehemently opposed by the adherents of that religion. They would protest that it is no man-made illusion, no dream produced by human needs and wishes, but instead has its source in God, being what no eye has seen, nor ear heard, nor (they would emphasize) the heart of men conceived. With the writers of *The Jerusalem Bible*'s Introduction to the Pentateuch, they would say: "The religion of the Old Testament, like that of the New, is a historical religion: it is based on a divine revelation made to definite individuals at definite times and in definite circumstances, on the intervention of God in history at specific moments of our human story."

It is this sort of stance by adherents that presents Freud with "a very remarkable psychological problem" (*FI*, p. 41). And it is to deal with this problem that he introduces the second of the two theses that I mentioned earlier, the one that concerns the individual believer's acceptance of the doctrines of the Christian religion.

III

What is the remarkable psychological problem Freud addresses himself to? It is this. We have a body of religious "ideas" that purportedly apprise us of ultimate matters: that there is a God who created the world and who cares for us, who knows our nature and our needs even better than we do, who has decreed "a moral order in the universe" and promised everlasting life to those who believe on his name. These ideas or doctrines have found wide acceptance and "have exercised the strongest possible influence on mankind." But they have done so *in spite of the fact that they have little or no authentication*. This is a remarkable state of affairs. With ideas of much less importance we demand authentication before giving assent to them. How is it, then, that when confronted by ideas that we regard as having the greatest importance we grow slack in our demands for authentication? One would naturally suppose that the greater the importance of a doctrine the more careful people would be about accepting it. But this, puzzlingly, is not borne out in the case of religious ideas. This is Freud's "remarkable psychological problem" (*FI*, pp. 37f.).

Freud's answer to it runs as follows. Religious ideas hold sway over us despite their lack of authentication because they are illusions. "What is characteristic of illusions is that they are derived from human wishes." Religious ideas are illusions that are "fulfilments of the oldest, strongest and most urgent wishes of mankind. The secret of their strength lies in the strength of those wishes" (*FI*, p. 47). That is, in brief, Freud's solution. And it is also a statement of what I have called his second thesis, the one concerning the reasons why individual believers accept Christianity. Freud's thesis is that believers embrace it (despite the lack of authentication) because of a deep, strong wish and need for love in a hard world. (Here we can see that Freud's two theses are Siamese twins, for by his account, both the origin of Judaeo-Christianity and the fact that it takes over people's lives lie in the operation of the same psychic mechanism: the illusion-producing wish.)

Consider now the following reaction to Freud's second thesis. "Freud seeks to explain why religious doctrines are believed even though they lack authentication. Put summarily, his explanation is that one believes them to be so because one *wants* them to be so. The pattern of explanation exemplified by this is a familiar one: A mother continues to believe that her son is not a shoplifter despite strong evidence to the contrary, and in explanation it is said that she *wants* him to be innocent. In another case, a professor continues to harbor no doubts that he will receive tenure even though it is clear to his colleagues that this is most unlikely. In a discussion of the professor's situation a colleague opines, 'He doesn't see that his chances are practically nil because he doesn't want to. He believes he'll get tenure just because he wants it so badly.' And this explanation is accepted.

"Such cases may serve to remind us that we do sometimes take a person's wishes and desires to determine what he believes. And so we must recognize that Freud's explanation of why religious believers believe follows a pattern that has a place in our lives. This is not to say, however, that Freud's explanation is acceptable. And in fact it is *not* acceptable. This can be seen if we elaborate the case of the untenured professor in a way that makes it parallel the case of the religious believer. (Let's call the professor 'Professor Z.')

"Professor Z happens to overhear his colleague say of him, 'He believes he'll get tenure just because he wants it so badly.' Professor Z steps in to respond. He says, 'No, you're wrong. I want tenure. That's true. But it's not *because* I want it that I have no doubt I'll get it. I'm sure I'll get it because I was assured months ago by the president himself that I will! A bomb-shell, eh?' " And Professor Z departs, leaving his colleagues with mouths agape.

"Now clearly if Professor Z has received the promise of tenure from the man at the top, the man empowered to grant it, then, if Z has no reason to doubt that the president will keep his promise, he has no reason to doubt that he will be tenured. And his colleagues's explanation of Z's assurance ('Z *wants* tenure') will have missed the mark. For though Z does want tenure, his certainty about getting it is clearly *not* due to this desire, but instead is based on the president's assurances.

"The case of Professor Z clearly parallels the case of the religious believer. For just as Professor Z's belief that he'll be tenured is based not on his desire but instead on the president's promise, so the believer's acceptance of doctrine is not caused by his wishes, but is instead based on his belief that God himself has, through the holy scriptures, assured him of its truth."

Will this response to Freud do? It may seem that it will, that the appeal to the doctrine of revelation obviates Freud's appeal to human needs and wishes. One may feel like saying to Freud, "Surely you can see that if you believed certain things which lacked 'authentication'—believed them because by your lights an unimpeachable authority assured you they were so, there would be no question *why* you believed them. So you see that there is no need to invoke a believer's *wishes;* only one of his *beliefs,* his belief in the doctrine of revelation, need be considered."

But Freud anticipates this response. He says that it does not help to have it asserted that the wording or content of the scriptures originates in divine revelation. "For this assertion is itself one of the doctrines whose authenticity is under examination. . . ." The point Freud wishes to make is this. The belief that *God has revealed* that he exists, created the world and so on is, despite being about the *origin* of the doctrines, just another religious doctrine whose hold on the believer (and indeed whose very existence) stems from humanity's deepest, most powerful wishes.

The appeal to revelation to explain why one believes religious doctrines seems thus to be unavailing. Freud appears to have trumped the believer's ace. I say *appears;* I do not think he has really done so. He has actually played a card of equal dialectical value. Neither Freud nor the believer takes the trick, and in fact neither of them wins the game. "But is there no objective character here?" Wittgenstein asks that question in his book *On Certainty.* And he answers by saying, "*Very* intelligent and well-educated people believe in the story of creation in the Bible, while others hold it as proven false, and the grounds of the latter are well known to the former." What I hope to show is that what Wittgenstein says here about the doctrine of creation goes also for the whole body of doctrine, where the very intelligent and well-educated people involved are believers and Freudians. Neither side wins the game.

IV

What is this game that neither Freud nor believer wins? What is its object? Its object is to provide the explanation of people's belief in the doctrines of Christianity without resorting to the thought that their belief is justified by evidence. But now, being unable to resort to this thought may seem a foolish restriction to some. They will say that the belief in question *is* justified by evidence, and it is silly for a believer to engage in a discussion with Freud in which this is assumed not to be so. It is to sit down to a game in which Freud has in effect simply been given the trick that in the end will assure him victory.

Not so, I reply! *Two* things here are not so. First, it is not true that belief in the doctrines is justified by evidence. This point, I realize, requires substantiation. Adequate consideration of the arguments for and against it, however, would require at least a chapter to itself. Perhaps it will be enough here to observe that many a nonbeliever knows the evidence (if that is what it is to be called) as well as, or better than many who believe. To turn around the remark just quoted from Wittgenstein: *Very* intelligent and well-educated people do not believe the story of creation in the Bible, while others hold it as proven true, and the grounds of the latter are well known to the former.

The other thing I wish to deny is this: that should the believer consent to play a game in which he cannot resort to the notion of justifying evidence, he will give Freud the winning trick. Half my thesis is that Freud does not win the game: he does not succeed in explaining to us why people believe the doctrines of Christianity.

But in saying that Freud does not win the explanation game, I do not wish to suggest that the believer wins it. The other half of my thesis is that he does not.

Let me try to make this clear by means of a famous narrative, Luke's account in Acts of Paul's experience on the road to Damascus. Up until the time of that experience Paul, then called "Saul," was a zealous persecutor of Christians, sending many of them, women and men, to prison in chains and even approving the stoning to death of Stephen. At one point, Luke tells us, Saul went to the high priest and asked for letters addressed to the synagogues in Damascus, authorizing him to arrest and take to

Jerusalem any Christians he could find. Luke's account continues in this way: "Suddenly, while he was travelling to Damascus and just before he reached the city, there came a light from heaven all round him. He fell to the ground, and then he heard a voice saying, 'Saul, Saul, why are you persecuting me?' 'Who are you, Lord?' he asked, and the voice answered, 'I am Jesus, and you are persecuting me. Get up now and go into the city, and you will be told what you have to do.' The men travelling with Saul stood there speechless, for though they heard the voice they could see no one. Saul got up from the ground, but even with his eyes wide open he could see nothing at all, and they had to lead him into Damascus by the hand. For three days he was without his sight, and took neither food nor drink."

As a result of this experience and the commission, subsequently delivered to him by Ananias, to bring the Lord's name before pagans as well as before the people of Israel, Paul's life was turned around. "I started preaching," he says, "first to the people of Damascus, then to those of Jerusalem and all the countryside of Judaea, and also to the pagans, urging them to repent and turn to God."

I do not know whether Freud wrote anything concerning this remarkable conversion. I think, however, that his general account of why people accept religious "ideas"—that they believe them true because they wish them to be true—warrants attributing something like the following to him: "Paul's visual and auditory experience on the road to Damascus, together with his belief that he had been addressed and commissioned by the risen Christ, are a return of the repressed—perhaps repressed feelings of guilt over his persecution of Christians. As his persecution of them was zealous, his fury extreme, so his guilt feelings were most anguishing and deep. And as they were auguishing and deep before repression, so they were on their return transformed, most spectacular: a vision and the hearing of a voice and the belief that a dead man, claimed to be the risen Son of God, had addressed him and made him an apostle. But the voice, as well as the rest, was only an irruption from his unconscious. The participants in that short conversation on the road were not Paul and one risen from the dead, but Paul and Paul."[3]

Now, our question is this: does such an account give us the answer to the question why Paul became a believer? And perhaps one may think, "Well, yes. *Some* such account is the answer. He was an epileptic, it is said. Perhaps generally unbalanced. The fury of his persecutions suggests this."

But let us consider another account.

> What the apostle [Paul] says is said with entire truthfulness, "Unto you it is given in the behalf of Christ not only to believe on Him, but also to suffer for His sake." He shows that both are the gifts of God, because he said that both are given. . . . [He knew] that he had been made faithful by God, who also had made him an apostle. For the beginnings of his faith are recorded . . .: how, being turned away from the faith which he was destroying, and being vehemently opposed to it, he was suddenly by a more powerful grace converted to it, by the conversion of [God] . . .; so that not only from one who refused to believe, he was made a willing believer, but, moreover, from being a persecutor, he suffered persecution in defence of that faith which he [had] persecuted. Because it was given him by Christ "not only to believe on Him, but also to suffer for his sake." [A *Treatise on the Predestination of the Saints*, chap. 4]

So here we have another answer, another explanation of Paul's belief. It was a gift of God. This is Paul's own thought as well as Saint Augustine's. And what Augustine says here of Paul's belief is the Christian explanation of the belief of all Christians.[4]

Who then wins the explanation game? Who provides the explanation of the believer's belief? Does Freud, when he says that belief is due to an unconscious wish? Or does the Christian explanation that belief is a gift of God win the day? I say neither wins.

Someone intervenes here on Freud's behalf: "But look. It is clearly just a shuffle to counter Freud's explanation of why Christians believe with the Christian's own, for the Christian's is merely *another* of those ideas or doctrines Freud accounts for. Freud is saying that it too, like the doctrine of revelation and the rest, is believed because of an unconscious wish. For although he does not mention it explicitly, it is certainly 'one of the doctrines whose authenticity is under examination.' And once this is realized, one will see the futility of trying to counter Freud's explanation with the Christian one. Freud's simply undercuts it. If *all* the apples in the barrel are rotten, it is no good going on saying, 'How about this one?—or that one?' Who then wins the explanation game? Consider. The Christian's last resort here is the doctrine that his believing, his faith, is a gift of God. But his belief that it is such a gift is itself to be explained as a product of deep needs and wishes. He thus can be seen to have *nothing* with which to resist Freud's pandoctrinal explanation, nothing to make us hesitate to award the garland of victory to Freud."

On the contrary, Freud deserves no victory garland. His explanation does not undercut the Christian one—not even when his explanation is applied to the Christian's *acceptance* of the Christian explanation by saying that the Christian's belief that faith is God's gift is itself to be explained as a product of deep needs and wishes. For the Christian's acceptance of this teaching concerning faith, his believing it, the Christian counts a part of the gift since his believing it is part of his faith. It is true that *if* all the apples in the barrel are rotten, it is no good going on saying, "How about this one?—or that one?" But there appears to be no reason to think that they are. Moreover, it is not even immediately clear that Freud himself thought they were—not at least if "All the apples are rotten" is a figurative way of saying "All the doctrines are false." Freud refrains from claiming their falsity by saying that one who believes them is under an illusion and that illusions, though they are produced by wishes, "need not necessarily be false" (*FI*, p. 49; cf. p. 52). Nevertheless, in claiming that believers believe because of an unconscious illusion-producing wish, Freud presupposes the falsity of one doctrine, the doctrine that teaches that God himself is the source of belief. If it is true that the source of belief is an unconscious wish, then it is not true that the source is God;[5] acceptance of Freud's naturalistic, atheistic explanation requires rejection of this theistic doctrine (just as acceptance of Freud's thesis concerning the origin of Judaeo-Christianity—that it was "born from man's need to make his helplessness tolerable"—requires rejection of the belief that Judaeo-Christianity has its origin in "the intervention of God in history at specific moments of our human story"). Freud, then, cannot consistently claim that the doctrine "need not necessarily be false," while claiming that the source of belief is an unconscious wish.

But the crucial point here is not that Freud is inconsistent; it is that in advancing his thesis that the source of belief is an unconscious wish he *just presupposes* the falsity of the doctrine that its source is God—that faith is God's gift (just as, it should here be pointed out, in advancing his thesis that Judaeo-Christianity was born from man's needs, he just presupposes the falsity of the doctrine that it has its origin in God's intervention in human history).

Again an intervention on Freud's behalf: "It is not true that Freud 'just presupposes' the falsity of either of these two doctrines. He alludes to a consideration—one that many besides him have noticed—which firmly supports this 'presupposition.' (And here it is clear that his thought comprehends not just the doctrines in question, but Judaeo-Christian doctrine as a whole.) Freud alludes to 'the fatal resemblance between religious ideas which we revere and the mental products of primitive peoples and times' (*FI*, p. 63). What Freud is pointing out is the following sort of thing: that, for example, at the time of Christ there were many besides him who claimed to be divine and whose followers claimed for them miraculous virgin birth. Here the religious ideas we revere—Christ's divinity and his virgin birth—are seen to resemble the mere 'mental products' of primitive peoples. And the resemblance, as Freud says, is fatal. No reasonable person can avoid concluding the falsity of those 'revered religious ideas.' In the name of informed straight thinking, they must be declared false once and for all!"

Now surely it must be admitted that informed straight thinking will find resemblances between Christian teachings and the acknowledged "mental products of primitive peoples." Informed but straighter thinking, however, will show that those resemblances are not fatal, that they do not show Christianity to be false. As any beginning logic student knows (to put the matter schematically): If case A and case B both have features *p*, *q*, *r*, and *s*, and if case A in addition has feature *f*, it does not follow that case B *also* has feature *f*. Thus in the case of Christianity: if at the time of Christ there were many men going around teaching and preaching and claiming they were divine, and if Christ too did these things, and if, further, the claim of these many to be divine were false, it does not follow that Christ's claim to be divine would be false. The resemblance, in other words, would not be fatal. And although it is not quite correct to say that Freud *just* presupposes the falsity of the doctrine that faith is God's gift, it is correct to say that the only "support" to be found in his book for that presupposition is the mere adumbration of a bad argument. And if he appears to beat the theist in the "game" of providing the explanation of why Christians believe, this appearance is due to his effort's being pervaded by this presupposition.

Here another spokesman for Freud intervenes: "Both you and my fellow Freudian interpret Freud's remark about fatal resemblances in the same way. By your interpretation the remark yields (I agree) a *bad* argument to the conclusion that Christianity is false. But there is another interpretation that yields a much stronger argument. In this interpretation the resemblance between revered religious ideas and primitive people's mental products is fatal, not in the sense that the resemblance shows those ideas to be false, but in the sense that it shows their acceptance to be at bottom arbitrary. The argument suggested is that a clear-headed, neutral inspection of the revered ideas and of the mental products reveals a crucial resemblance such that there is no justification for accepting one as true and rejecting the other as false. Acceptance of one over the other, then, is arbitrary. It is in this way, I think, that Freud speaks of a resemblance that is fatal."

There are three points requiring clarification in this argument. First, in speaking of "a crucial resemblance such that there is no justification," and so on, the argument may mislead. One may gain the impression that for Freud there are no significant differences between primitive mental products and the revered ideas. But Freud claims "a long process of development" of religious ideas and counts the rise of monotheism from polytheism of signal importance in that development. Now a religious pilgrim, a seeker, may also find such differences significant; he may find religious ideas in their "developed" form vastly more attractive, more nearly acceptable, than in their "undeveloped" form. C. S. Lewis was such a pilgrim. At one point in his journey, recounted in *Surprised by Joy,* he allows that the question was then for him "no longer to find the one simply true religion among a thousand religions simply false. It was rather, 'Where has religion reached its true maturity? Where, if anywhere, have the hints of all Paganism been fulfilled?' . . . Paganism had been only the childhood of religion, or only a prophetic dream. Where was the thing full grown? or where was the awakening?"

The differences, the development, can be seen as maturation, the fulfillment of hints; so that, as was the case with Lewis, who became a Christian convert, the mature forms, not the childish, attract and are the more nearly acceptable. Of course, to be the more attractive, the more nearly acceptable, is not to be actually acceptable, acceptable as *true.* Thus the central point of the

Freudian argument remains unblunted. It can allow that the revered ideas are mature and attractive, the primitives' mental products childish. For its real point is that, however mature and attractive they may be, the revered ideas so resemble the mental products that there is no justification for embracing them as the truth, that to do so is after all quite arbitrary.

This brings us to the second point requiring clarification. The argument tells us that however mature and attractive, the revered ideas so resemble the primitives' mental products that actually accepting them as true is arbitrary. But if accepting them is to be thought arbitrary, in what way must they resemble the primitives' mental products? How must the two be alike? The relevant point of resemblance must be just that ***both lack a reliable indication of truth.*** *No* religion, whether primitive or mature, contains a reliable indication of its truth. All resemble one another in this respect.

We can now examine the third point in need of clarification. If there is no reliable indication of truth in *any* religion, primitive or mature, so that choice must be arbitrary, then one's choice will be arbitrary whether one confronts several religions or only one. The number of religions confronting one is immaterial. The Freudian argument makes it appear that resemblances and comparisons are essential. The sole essential thing, however, whether in several cases or only in one, is to see that there is no reliable indication of truth.

What, then, is the point of the Freudian claim that there is a fatal resemblance between the revered ideas and the primitives' mental products? Only that since in the revered ideas, as (incidentally) in the mental products, there is no reliable indication of truth, choosing or accepting or embracing them as true is arbitrary.

If this is the point of the Freudian claim, what shall we say of it? Convinced of the unsuccess of the theological proofs of God's existence, many people, including some believers, will agree that the claim is true. There is no proof, they will say, of Christianity's truth or even of God's existence, and so to accept it as true is to make a leap in the dark. No bridge of reason spans the chasm; a leap of faith is required. And of course there may be no chasm: one may be leaping off land's end. Arbitrary? Yes, indeed.

This acquiescence in the Freudian claim is, however, too quick. Consider the following exchange in an interview of C. S. Lewis concerning his own conversion:

> *Mr. Wirt:* In your book *Surprised by Joy* you remark that you were brought into the Faith kicking and struggling and resentful, with eyes darting in every direction looking for an escape. You suggest that you were compelled, as it were, to become a Christian. Do you feel that you made a decision at the time of your conversion?
>
> *Lewis:* I would not put it that way. What I wrote in *Surprised by Joy* was that "before God closed in on me, I was in fact offered what now appears a moment of wholly free choice." But I feel my decision was not so important. I was the object rather than the subject in this affair. I was decided upon.[6]

Lewis would, it appears, agree with the Freudian claim that in the revered ideas there is no reliable indication of truth, no successful proof, no bridge of reason across the chasm. He would deny, however, that in embracing Christianity he made an arbitrary choice, for he would deny that at the crucial moment he made a choice at all. "I was the object rather than the subject in this affair. I was decided upon." He would say that he did not leap the chasm, but that he was yanked across it.[7]

This account of Lewis's conversion accords well with central scriptural pronouncements concerning choice in such matters. Jesus tells his disciples, "You did not choose me, no, I chose you" (John 15:16). And the Jews are told, "You are a people consecrated to Yahweh your God; it is you that Yahweh our God has chosen to be his very own people out of all the peoples of the earth" (Deut. 7:6).

Did the convert make an arbitrary choice? It seems that he chooses without reliable indications that what he chooses is true. And so his choice is arbitrary. But does he at the crucial moment choose at all? If not, then the accusation of arbitrariness cannot rightly fall on him. A says: "Silly! You leaped in the dark!" B replies: "I didn't leap, I was yanked! It was awful!" Freud says nothing that shows that B wasn't yanked.

I find nothing in Freud's two theses or in his development of them that requires discarding of the Christian doctrines his theses call into question—that is, the doctrine concerning the origin of the doctrines and that concerning why a Christian believes them. Moreover, anyone who, like John Maynard Keynes, deems Christianity obviously false is thinking badly if he cites Freud's book as his support. But I believe I should have said he's thinking badly in any case. Christianity is *not* obviously false. *Very* intelligent and well-educated people believe Christianity true, while others hold it as proven false, and the grounds of the latter are well known to the former. "What is more," one of those former might add, "the object of Keynes's abuse, Henry Sidgwick, who 'never did anything but wonder whether Christianity was true,' was really in the end the wiser man. For at least *he* hadn't slammed the door shut on the possibility of Life."

3 /

Two of Kierkegaard's Uses of "Paradox"

IN the span of a few pages of his *Concluding Unscientific Postscript** Soren Kierkegaard makes important use of the notion of paradox to distinguish two sorts of religiousness. I propose to study this notion as he employs it in characterizing the two.

The first sort he discusses is exemplified by the religiousness of Socrates and is what in other places he calls religiousness A. Regarding religiousness in this sense, Kierkegaard writes, "the eternal and essential truth, the truth which has an essential relation to an existing individual because it pertains essentially to existence . . . is a paradox. But the eternal essential truth is by no means in itself a paradox; but it becomes paradoxical by virtue of its relation to an existing individual" (*PS*, p. 183).

The second sort of religiousness is exemplified by Christianity and is what Kierkegaard elsewhere calls religiousness *B*. He distinguishes the two sorts in the following passage:

> Subjectivity is truth. By virtue of the relationship subsisting be-

*Translated by David F. Swenson and Walter Lowrie (Princeton: Princeton University Press, 1941), pp. 177–188. All subsequent references in this chapter to *Concluding Unscientific Postscript* will be abbreviated to *PS*, followed by the page number.

> tween the eternal truth and the existing individual, the paradox came into being. Let us now go further, let us suppose that the eternal essential truth is itself a paradox. How does the paradox come into being? By putting the eternal essential truth into juxtaposition with existence. Hence when we posit such a conjunction within the truth itself, the truth becomes a paradox. [*PS*, p. 187]

So far then we have the following picture. There is a paradox involved in the first sort of religiousness, a paradox that arises from the fact that the existing individual, the believer, is related essentially to the eternal essential truth. The second sort of religiousness is distinguished by the presence of a second paradox in addition to the first: "the eternal essential truth is itself a paradox."

I

The paradox in the first sort of religiousness involves the concepts *truth* and *objective uncertainty*. We may show what these concepts involve by making use of one of Kierkegaard's illustrations.

> When one man investigates objectively the problem of immortality, and another embraces an uncertainty with the passion of the infinite: where is there most truth, and who has the greater certainty? The one has entered upon a never-ending approximation, for the certainty of immortality lies precisely in the subjectivity of the individual; the other is immortal, and fights for his immortality by struggling with the uncertainty. [*PS*, p. 180]

Here two sorts of people are contrasted: one who seeks objective certainty or proof of the soul's immortality but is necessarily embarked "upon a never-ending approximation" and the other who is certain, for he has embraced the uncertainty with the passion of the infinite, and "the certainty of immortality lies precisely in the subjectivity of the individual." Kierkegaard continues thus:

> Let us consider Socrates. Nowadays everyone dabbles in a few proofs; some have several such proofs, others fewer. But Socrates! He puts the question objectively in a problematic manner: *if* there is an immortality. He must therefore be accounted a doubter in comparison with one of our modern thinkers with the three proofs? By no means. On this "if" he risks his entire life, he has the courage to meet death, and he has with the passion of the infinite so determined the pattern of his life that it must be found acceptable—*if* there is an immortality. Is any better proof capable of being given for the immortality of the soul? But those who have the three proofs do not at all determine their lives in conformity therewith; if there is an immortality it must feel disgust over their manner of life: can any better refutation be given of the three proofs? The bit of uncertainty Socrates had, helped him because he himself contributed the passion of the infinite; the three proofs that the others have do not profit them at all, because they are dead to spirit and enthusiasm, and their three proofs, in lieu of proving anything else, prove just this. . . . The Socratic ignorance, which Socrates held fast with the entire passion of his inwardness, was thus an expression for the principle that the eternal truth is related to an existing individual, and that this truth must therefore be a paradox for him as long as he exists. [*PS*, p. 180].

In the above passage one can see what the concepts of objective uncertainty and truth are. Objective uncertainty is the *if* of Socrates. He does not *know* whether his soul is immortal, but *if* it is . . . On the other hand, truth—the certainty of Socrates—is shown in this: that "he has with the passion of the infinite so determined the pattern of his life that it must be found acceptable."

Second, the above passage shows, though not very clearly, the way in which the notion of paradox is involved with the concepts of objective uncertainty and truth. As Kierkegaard puts it here, "The Socratic ignorance [that is, Socrates' objective uncertainty], which Socrates held fast with the entire passion of his inwardness, was thus an expression for the principle that the eternal truth is related to an existing individual, and that this truth must therefore be a paradox for him as long as he exists." Another passage makes clearer the relation between the notion of paradox and the concepts of objective uncertainty and truth: "When subjectivity, inwardness, is the truth, the truth becomes objectively a paradox; . . . The paradoxical character of the [subjective, inward] truth is its objective uncertainty" (*PS*, p. 183). Thus in the case of Socrates the paradox enters in this way: whereas Socrates is subjectively *certain* that he is immortal (and this is shown in "the pattern of his life"), still he is objectively *uncertain* that he is immortal. To paraphrase the second of the two sentences quoted above: the paradoxical character of Socrates' "certainty," his "subjective truth," is its objective uncertainty, or his objective uncertainty of it. The paradox is that he is at once certain and uncertain—certain subjectively and uncertain objectively. What might be called the logic of this notion of paradox is perhaps made clearer in the following.

Suppose a woman and her child live in a house in one room of which there is possibly a poisonous snake. The snake has never been seen *in* the room, but the woman once saw it outside the house, apparently about to crawl through a hole into the room. She did not, however, see it actually enter. Further, though she has never seen the snake in the room, there are many places where it might hide there, and at night she has heard queer noises that come, perhaps, from the room.

Now the woman does nothing. Yet she fears snakes terribly, and it is not as though she is embarrassed to ask someone to search the room—anyone would understand her fear of snakes and her wanting to make certain in this case. But she does nothing. Moreover, she conducts her life as though there were no possibility of a poisonous snake's being in the room. She sends her child to the room to get thread; she goes there herself and rummages in the closets for extra blankets when the night turns cold.

Noticing how she conducts herself, someone asks her, "What

makes you so sure that there is no snake in that room?" She replies, "Oh, but I'm *not* sure. Would you be sure? For, as you know, I saw the snake outside near the hole, and at night I've heard noises." "But then," responds the other, amazed, "if you're *not* sure, how can you *live* in such assurance!" "But don't you see," comes the reply, "I believe that the snake is not there."

This case exhibits the logic of "paradox" as Kierkegaard brings that word into his discussion of Socrates and immortality.[1] The woman is "objectively uncertain"; that is, she is not sure whether or not the snake is in the room and can give reasons that would lead anyone to be unsure and to want to make sure. Yet she is subjectively certain; that is, she lives just as though she had made sure there was no snake in the room.

It is safe to say that one would meet such a woman only in fiction, and not even there if the fiction was worth reading. For if one tried to imagine her life in detail, insurmountable problems would arise. What, for instance, does she do when in bed at night she hears the strange noises that *might* be those of the snake? If she believes, as she says, that the snake is not in the room, that is, if she *lives* in the assurance that the snake is not there, then her reaction to the noise also must express this assurance. And so when she cites as a reason for being uncertain the fact that she has heard the strange noise, one can only suppose that she is not taking her "reason" seriously as a reason and so she is not really uncertain. Or if she does take her reason seriously as a reason, then when she hears the noise she shudders in fear and repulsion, or she frets, "I wonder if that's that snake"—in which case she does not believe, she does not live in assurance.

Now to say that insurmountable problems arise if one tries to imagine in detail the life of this woman is to say that no such life can be imagined, let alone lived—not because even the geniuses of fiction are not equal to the task, but because it makes no sense to say of a person, real or fictional, that he is objectively uncertain and also subjectively certain. The facts which would justify our saying that a person is objectively uncertain are the very facts which would justify our saying that he is not subjectively certain, and vice versa.

What I wish to argue is this: there is nothing in the case of the person in religiousness A that can be called a paradox in the sense in which there is one in the case of the woman, even though Kierkegaard supposes that there is.

"The paradoxical character of the truth is its objective uncertainty." So says Kierkegaard. And to the case of the woman this sentence applies perfectly. For without the "objective uncertainty," that is, with objective certainty, there is no paradox—and then we can make sense of her case. In religiousness A, however, there is nothing like the woman's "objective uncertainty," nothing like what we might naturally understand by that phrase, nothing like what Kierkegaard himself, at least sometimes, understands by it.

How then does Kierkegaard understand the phrase "objective uncertainty"? He understands it as involving the concept of evidence, as it does in the case of the woman. The following passage indicates this: "I contemplate the order of nature in the hope of finding God, and I see omnipotence and wisdom; but I also see much else that disturbs my mind and excites anxiety. The sum of all this is objective uncertainty" (*PS*, p. 182). This is like: "I contemplate the evidence in the hope of finding him innocent, and I see that he can pretty well account for his time on the day of the crime and that he has little motive; but I also see much else that disturbs my mind and excites anxiety. The sum of all this is objective uncertainty." Thus we see that here for Kierkegaard the concept of objective uncertainty is connected with the notion of evidence for and evidence against.[2] And of course when one has both kinds of evidence, then the evidence is said to be inconclusive and one is uncertain.

One can now see pretty clearly how Kierkegaard comes to think that a paradox is involved in religiousness A. One contemplates the order of nature, finds evidence both for and against saying there is a God, sees the evidence to be inconclusive, becomes (objectively) uncertain, and then—despite his uncertainty—is (subjectively) certain there is a God. But, as in the case of the woman and the snake, when this is considered in detail the nonsense involved becomes evident. For if one is subjectively certain, that is, if he lives assured that he is in God's hands, then when he is confronted with what he regards as evidence for the nonexistence of God, he must either be disturbed and so not be in assurance, or remain in assurance and so not be taking the "evidence" seriously as evidence.

It is perhaps surprising that Kierkegaard should have introduced the concept of objective uncertainty in this way at all. For in other places he insists that "Christianity is not a matter of knowledge, so that increased knowledge is of no avail, except to make it easier to fall into the confusion of considering Christianity as a matter of knowledge."[3] I take it that this goes for religiousness A as well as for Christianity. Now if Christianity or religiousness A "is not a matter of knowledge, so that increased knowledge is of no avail," then *it is not a matter of objective uncertainty either.* For saying that it is not a matter of knowledge, and so on, is not to say that we do not as a matter of fact know something or other and so are uncertain; it is to say that knowing *and* not knowing (hence, being uncertain) are irrelevant.

Thus for Kierkegaard (at this place in the *Postscript*) the concept *knowledge* is irrelevant to the faith relationship; that is, such a sentence as "I know that God exists," where knowing involves finding out or making proofs, brings together concepts which on coming together curdle into nonsense. But he is not clear that the irrelevancy he is claiming involves also the irrelevancy of the concept of objective uncertainty; that is, that such a sentence as "I am (objectively) uncertain that God exists" likewise brings together concepts that curdle on contact into nonsense.[4]

My argument here is this: religion, Kierkegaard claims, is not a matter of knowledge. If this is true, then religion is not a matter of objective uncertainty either. And if it is not a matter of objective uncertainty, then there is no paradox, since there being a paradox depends on religion's being a matter of objective uncertainty.

II

Before turning to the paradox distinguishing religiousness *B* from religiousness A, we must consider an objection to the foregoing critique. The objection is this. "It is a mistake to take the claim that religiousness A is not a matter of knowledge such that it is also not a matter of objective uncertainty. Whatever Kierkegaard's claim may come to, his reliance on the notion of objective uncertainty is too important to his position to be dismissed in this way. What he means by 'objective uncertainty' is made quite clear in the passage, already cited, in which he speaks of contemplating the order of nature and seeing omnipotence and wisdom but also much else that distrubs the mind and excites anxiety. 'The sum of all this,' he says, 'is objective uncertainty.'

"Objective uncertainty, so understood [the objection continues], is integral to religiousness A, to man's relationship to God. So long as a man lives he cannot be objectively certain of God's existence. Contemplating the order of nature can never resolve the uncertainty; what disturbs his mind and excites anxiety will always be there. Moreover, it is this objective uncertainty that produces or constitutes the risk that Kierkegaard rightly considers the *sine qua non* of faith (*PS*, p. 182). Thus in a man's proper relationship to God both subjective certainty (faith) and objective uncertainty, with its disturbance of mind and anxiety, must be present. It is this that constitutes the paradox of religiousness A."

If this presentation of Kierkegaard's position is not to be vulnerable, as the earlier presentation is, to reduction to absurdity by means of the woman and snake case, we must understand subjective certainty and objective uncertainty in one of three ways.

(1) Objective uncertainty with its disturbance and anxiety *interrupts* one's subjective certainty each time one honestly considers the order of nature, which is impenetrably ambiguous.

(2) Objective uncertainty describes only the situation's, not the believer's, condition. The order of nature is ambiguous, yielding no conclusive evidence either for or against, but yielding partial evidence both for and against, the proposition that God exists. Objective uncertainty's psychological aspect, the disturance of mind and anxiety, is here absent. Thus in the face of nature's ambiguousness it is possible for the believer to maintain an uninterrupted subjective certainty.

(3) Objective uncertainty, including its psychological aspect, is a constant conditioner of subjective certainty with the result that subjective certainty is not after all the conviction, but is instead the hope, that God exists.[5]

Interpretation (1) seems to make the believer remarkably slack-souled and self-deceived. Whenever he considers the ambiguous order of nature, he is assailed by disturbing and anxious doubts about God's existence, but when this ambiguity is out of sight his doubts are out of mind and certainty floods in again, allowing him to pray to God in perfect confidence that God is there to hear—until of course it is time for another assessment of the evidence. He must, it seems, make frequent reassessments of the evidence, for he must "constantly be intent on holding fast the objective uncertainty" (*PS*, p. 182). But despite these efforts doubt falls asleep, certainty returns, and the believer can again live, unconscionably, beyond his evidential means.

Can this be Kierkegaard's portrait of the believer? Surely not. For one thing Kierkegaard's believer does not oscillate between subjective certainty and the anxious doubts of objective uncertainty. Instead, both the subjective and the objective elements are somehow constantly present. The beliver is in fact to intensify his subjective certainty by vigilantly maintaining a constant objective uncertainty. Kierkegaard would not promote the ideal of an oscillating belief, which to call it by its right name is nothing but inconstancy.

But if in Kierkegaard's portrait both subjective and objective elements are constantly present, is that portrait not again vulnerable to the *reductio* of the woman and snake case? Is it not correct to say of the believer's as well as the woman's case that the facts that would justify saying that a person is objectively uncertain are the very facts that would justify saying that he is *not* subjectively certain, and vice versa?

Interpretation (2) avoids this *reductio* as well as the objectionable oscillation in interpretation (1). In the second interpretation the psychological aspect (the anxieties and doubt) of objective uncertainty is absent. It is the situation, not the believer, that is uncertain. He maintains a subjective certainty uninterrupted by by doubts fostered by nature's ambiguity. Presumably he manages to do this by simply ignoring the ambiguity.

This interpretation of Kierkegaard's portrait of the believer seems as objectionable as our first one. It invites invidious but apparently unavoidable comparisons: the believer is like a police detective who remains convinced that Mrs. B is guilty of murdering her sister only because he ignores evidence that makes this doubtful; or the believer is like a cancer sufferer who remains convinced that Laetrile cures cancer because he ignores evidence that makes this doubtful; or (to adapt our woman and snake case) the believer is like the woman who remains free of all doubt that the room is safe just because she ignores two important facts: first, that though she did not see the snake actually enter the room, she saw it outside the house, apparently about to crawl through a hole into the room, and, second, that at night, when the house is quiet, she hears strange noises coming, perhaps, from the room, noises that might be made by the snake.

Under our first interpretation Kierkegaard's believer is slack and inconstant. Under our second he is intellectually irresponsible, and the fact that nature's impenetrable ambiguity renders conclusive evidence unattainable constitutes no mitigation of this irresponsibility. A freedom from doubt maintained by ignoring contrary evidence is despicable whether or not conclusive evidence can be attained.

Interpretation (3) escapes both difficulties. Here the believer is neither inconstant nor irresponsible. His objective uncertainty is such that he understands the risk involved in being subjectively certain of God's existence. He understands that certainty is not justified by the evidence. He is not intellectually irresponsible, he does not live beyond his evidential means. His subjective certainty, then, is not the conviction, but is instead the hope, that God exists. And since contrary evidence need touch only the conviction, the hope may remain steady, the believer thereby avoiding inconstancy.

On this interpretation are there other difficulties? The believer understands that nature's ambiguous face does not afford conclusive evidence of God's existence, that it affords some evidence to the contrary. Thus he is not convinced that God exists, but he hopes so and on the basis of this hope lives *as though* it is true that God exists.

To examine this interpretation let us again adapt the woman and snake case. The woman is not convinced that the room is safe, yet she hopes that it is and on the basis of this hope lives her life as though it is true that it is. Hoping that the snake has not entered, she goes into the room and rummages in the closet for household items and sends her child there for the shoes she has left under the bed. Is her search for blankets a bit rushed and perfunctory? Does she glance anxiously about? Does she step gingerly? Is she apprehensive about her child's safety? No. She lives as though it is true that the snake is not in the room. To a neighbor who knows what the woman has seen outside the house and what she hears in the dead of night and who consequently is puzzled at her lack of fear and concern, she explains that her equanimity is due to her hope that the snake is not in the room.

Clearly, hope is no explanation of the woman's behavior. The arithmetic is bad. Realization of the grave risk plus hope that the snake is not in the room does not add up to perfect equanimity. But though bad in the woman's case, perhaps the same arithmetic is correct in the believer's. The risk may seem far less grave here. The believer realizes only that God may not exist—a realization not nearly as distrubing, one may think, as that a poisonous snake may lie hidden in a bedroom of one's house. Does this realization plus the hope that God exists equal the analogue of the woman's equanimity? Do we understand a life of faith that is lived on the basis of the hope, not the conviction, that God exists?

The life of faith is a life lived to fulfill the Commandments, the chief of which, believers are taught, is to love the Lord your God with all your heart, with all your soul, and with all your mind. One important expression of this love is understood to be prayer: for example praise and declarations of love like these:

> I love thee, O Lord, my strength.
> The Lord is my rock and my fortress, and my deliverer, . . .
> [Ps. 18:1–2]

> O my Strength, I will sing praises to thee,
> for thou, O God, art my fortress,
> the God who shows me steadfast love. [Ps. 59:17]

Surely in reading these verses it will not do to imagine in the psalmist only the hope and not the conviction that God exists! Surely the serious believer, who tries to conform his life to the Commandments, cannot be thought merely to hope that God exists. Kierkegaard himself seems to agree. He writes: "Do away with the terrors of eternity (either eternal happiness or eternal perdition) and the idea of an imitation of Christ is fantastic. Only the seriousness of eternity can compel and move a man to take such a daring decision and answer for his so doing. . . . It must be a question of heaven or hell—and of imitating him for that reason *i.e.* to be saved: that is seriousness" (*Journals*, X¹ A452). What are the terrors of eternity to one who is not even convinced of their existence?

Furthermore, believers are instructed that they must believe, not that they must hope, that God exists: "For whoever would draw near to God must believe [the word is not "hope"] that he exists and that he rewards those who seek him" (Heb. 11:6).

The arithmetic seems no better in the believer's case than it is in the woman's. The realization that God may not exist plus the hope that He does exist cannot add up to a life of faith. To think that it does is to be prepared to think that when Simone Weil penned her account of her mystical experience (see Chap. 2, note 7), after finishing its culminating sentence—"And it happened that as I was saying this poem . . . Christ himself came down, and He took me"—she ought really to have added self-reprovingly, "Of course I ought only to have *hoped* it was He!"

In any attempt to repel the supposed encroachment of nature's ambiguity on the intelligibility or intellectual respectability of religious belief, it is a strategic error to establish the battle line at the hope that God exists. If that is done the battle is lost. It seems that the line must be established farther forward at the conviction or belief that he exists. But is the battle not lost if fought here as well? Haven't we already seen it lost here to the charges of logical absurdity, inconstancy, or intellectual irresponsibility? If the life of faith requires the conviction that God exists, there seems no way the believer can avoid the charge of irresponsibility at least. For the evidence that nature affords simply does not justify that conviction.

At this point one may feel that the battle is lost: that the life of faith is really intellectually irresponsible because evidentially underfunded and that Kierkegaard's claim of "paradox" is the Grand Mystifier's way of alluding to that irresponsibility while at the same time trying to keep us, and no doubt himself as well, from seeing the irresponsibility for what it is.

On the other hand, one may feel that Kierkegaard's portrait of the believer has somehow placed us in that notorious Wittgensteinian room on one wall of which is painted a series of dummy doors and that we have all this while been fumbling at one after another of those doors trying to find an exit and have only to turn around to see the real way out.

Let us try turning around. To do this we must reject the notion that the believer irresponsibly ignores the insufficiency of the evidence nature affords. Of course we must not do this by claiming that the evidence is after all sufficient. Instead, we must do it by understanding that the believer does not come to the conviction that God exists by *concluding* to it—either responsibly or irresponsibly. The psalmist who declares the heavens to be the work of God's fingers is not "announcing his findings." He is not, then, irresponsibly ignoring contrary evidence in nature, for nature is not evidence in his enterprise. His conviction arises quite otherwise.[6]

If the conviction that God exists does not arise in the serious man of faith through an assessment, or misassessment, of the order of nature, then how does it arise? What Hume once wrote, though hostile to belief and ironic in intention, actually comes very close to Belief's own answer to this question. At the end of the discussion of miracles in his *Inquiry Concerning Human Understanding* he wrote:

> So that upon the whole we may conclude, that the *Christian Religion* not only was at first attended with miracles, but even to this day cannot be believed by any reasonable person without one. Mere reason is not sufficient to convince us of its veracity: and

whoever is moved by ***Faith*** to assent to it, is conscious of a continued miracle in his own person.

Does Hume's remark indicate a way out of the Wittgensteinian room? If we ignore its irony the remark suggests that in the serious man of faith the conviction that God exists is established by God, by miracle.

Saint Paul, in his first letter to the Corinthians (2:14) suggests the same thing when he says that "an unspiritual person," that is, one "left to his own natural resources,"[7] "does not accept anything of the Spirit of God" and that such a person "sees it all as nonsense." Understanding and acceptance come only "by means of the Spirit." Paul is suggesting that the "message of the Kingdom," in which with much else is revealed the King's existence, can be believed only by one who is prepared by God's Spirit to do so. This preparation, this spiritualizing of the natural man that enables him to believe, is the miracle that Hume, himself unbelieving, ironically spoke of.

It seems that at this point it is not open to the unbeliever to speak otherwise than ironically. An unbeliever cannot accept the believer's account of how the conviction of God's existence arises. If he did, he would not be an unbeliever. Is the unbeliever then forced to accept the account we have already rejected—that the conviction is concluded to from (insufficient) evidence found in the order of nature? No; one need not be a believer in order to see that no concluding, no announcing one's findings, is involved. But are not "miracle" and "insufficient evidence with intellectual irresponsibility" the only alternatives available? Again, no; there is at least the additional alternative of silence, of having no account to give. In fact it seems to be to Hume's credit that in the passage quoted he gives no account and instead contents himself with scoffing.[8]

We have now examined Kierkegaard's portrait of the believer. The puzzling aspect of that portrait is the claim that the believer is both objectively uncertain and subjectively certain that God exists. We first argued by means of the woman and snake case that this claim involved logical absurdity, for the facts justifying an affirmation of objective uncertainty are the very ones that justify a denial of subjective certainty, and vice versa. We then considered three "interpretations" of Kierkegaard's portrait, finding each to sustain a different serious objection: the first, inconstancy; the second, intellectual irresponsibility; the third, the absence of the conviction that God exists.

We then presented a portrait of the believer that avoids all of the above objections. But in our portrait he is not "objectively uncertain" of God's existence. He does not harbor that "bit of uncertainty" that Kierkegaard finds in Socrates and gives to his believer. Nor does the ambiguity of nature's face leave our believer's conviction that God exists evidentially underfunded. The situation's "objective uncertainty" is irrelevant. In his enterprise nature is not evidence.

What then becomes of Kierkegaard's claim that a paradox is involved in religiousness A? It seems that since there is no place for a Kierkegaardian objective uncertainty, there is none for a paradox, because paradox arises only out of a conjunction of subjective certainty with that objective uncertainty.

Before concluding this section, we must consider briefly how our disposition of the difficulty in Kierkegaard's portrait of the believer bears on a well-known fact of religious life: the vicissitudes, the infirmity, of faith. This infirmity I will here refer to as doubt.

Doubt admits of degrees of seriousness, ranging from double-mindedness to apostasy. There is the occasional visitation of profane thoughts, such perhaps as those evil thoughts against whose violent incursions Dr. Johnson petitioned God's defense. There is also that condition of religious melancholia, called *accidia* or sloth, in which, as Evelyn Waugh describes it in *The Seven Deadly Sins*, "a man is fully aware of the proper means of his salvation and refuses to take them because the whole apparatus of salvation fills him with tedium and disgust." This seems close to the condition Graham Greene describes in his autobiography, *A Sort of Life*: "we may become hardened to the formulas of Confession and skeptical about ourselves; we may only half intend to keep the promises we make, until continual failure or the circumstances of our private life finally make it impossible to make any promises at all and many of us abandon Confession and Communion to join the Foreign Legion of the Church and fight for a city of which we are no longer full citizens."

But of course doubt can take a more deadly form, that of perfect indifference of the heart. This is the doubt of the *pococurante*, whose attitude H. H. Price characterizes in "Faith and Belief"[9] by letting him speak out: "Oh, yes, of course there is a God and of course he loves every one of us, and no doubt he asks each one of us to love him. But what of it?" The *pococurante* approaches but does not quite reach apostasy, for though he cares nothing about it, he refrains from denying or questioning God's existence.

The apostate passes Dr. Johnson's evil thoughts, Waugh's *accidia*, Greene's foreign legionnaire, and Price's *pococurante;* he does not stop at tedium or indifference to God. He scoffs at the notion of God's existence.

This sampling of religious doubting, or defection, can at best only suggest its many forms. Indeed, it may not be amiss here to adapt a famous sentence of Tolstoy's: Firm believers are all alike; every doubter doubts in his own way. Yet one may wonder too whether firm believers can be separated in this way from doubters. Perhaps to apostasy's deepest doubt even the firmest believer is not always immune. Perhaps some of those evil thoughts that so appalled Dr. Johnson were, in whatever form, doubts of God's existence, doubts against which, like a man trying to hang on, Johnson appealed to God for protection.

Suppose, then, that no believer-doubter completely escapes the apostate's doubt; suppose that even the psalmist's firm and abiding conviction of God's existence is sometimes, however fleetingly, clouded by what the fool says in his heart.

Despite one plausible reading of Kierkegaard, such doubt, however unavoidable, is the believer's shame, not his glory. If that doubt is what Kierkegaard was calling objective uncertainty, it is emphatically not something the believer thinks he must "constantly be intent on holding fast."

More importantly, this doubt is not something he should think he finds evidence in nature to support. Just as in declaring the heavens to be the work of God's fingers the psalmist is not announcing his findings, so the doubt that God exists and created the heavens is not the product of further research. Instead, as Kierkegaard observes in a *Journal* entry (VIII A 7) that is at once a piece of profound religious psychology and an important delimiting conceptual remark, the doubts of a faltering faith are really objections that "spring from insubordination, the dislike of obedience, rebellion against all authority"—not, then, the intellect, dissuaded by counterevidence, weakening or abandoning its "God-hypothesis"; but the will or spirit enfeebled, perhaps in circumstances too hard, or not hard enough, failing like five foolish virgins.

III

Let us now turn to the paradox which distinguishes religiousness *B* from religiousness A. To study this paradox, let us focus on Kierkegaard's discussion of the story of Abraham and Isaac. Though I know of no place in Kierkegaard's writings where he explicitly says that Abraham is in religiousness *B*, there is much in his work that naturally leads one to think that he *would* have said so. The category of the absurd, for example, has office in religiousness *B* but not in religiousness A; also faith in its highest sense pertains to religiousness *B* but not in its highest sense to religiousness A (*PS*, pp. 183–184 and 187–188). Now the category of the absurd plays a major role in Kierkegaard's characterization of the religion of Abraham, and also Kierkegaard's passionate interest in the Abraham story results from his regarding it as exhibiting the archetype of the faithful man. In addition to these considerations, there is also the authority of Walter Lowrie, the scholar-translator of Kierkegaard's works. In one of his "translator's notes" to his translation of *Fear and Trembling*, he writes: "It is Johannes de silentio who says [that he cannot understand Abraham] and the purpose of [saying this] is to emphasize the fact that the paradoxical religiousness (religiousness B) is and remains a paradox to everyone who stands on a lower plane."[10]

This note, in addition to the considerations concerning faith and the absurd, seems sufficient warrant for regarding Abraham as one who, for Kierkegaard, is in "the paradoxical religion" and for allowing our analysis of the paradox in Abraham's case to stand as an analysis of the paradox that distinguishes religiousness *B* from religiousness A.

It has been contended that by "paradox" in the case of religiousness *B* Kierkegaard means "logical contradiction" or "logical impossibility," and there is much in Kierkegaard's writing that might easily be taken to support this view. In fact Kierkegaard does use the word "contradiction" to refer to the paradox.[11] The remainder of this chapter will be devoted to a consideration of this question: does the paradox of religiousness *B*, as it is exemplified in the case of Abraham, involve a logical contradiction or impossibility? Is there, in other words, a logical impossibility involved in this paradox: that Abraham intended to obey God's command to *sacrifice* Isaac while at the same time believing that God's promise to him would be fulfilled—the promise that *through Isaac* his seed should be multiplied as the stars of the heaven? In examining this paradox I shall bear in mind Kierkegaard's warning that the paradox cannot be understood (*PS*, pp. 196–197). I will not try to explain away the paradox, to resolve it, but only to make clear what Kierkegaard is calling a paradox.

To help us in characterizing what Kierkegaard calls a paradox we shall consider the following case, which is similar in some respects to Abraham's. An army private has received his company commander's promise of a pass for the following weekend. He will spend the weekend in a nearby town. The day after receiving the promise he is informed that the company commander has chosen him to do guard duty on the weekend covered by the promise. The private casually mentions this state of affairs to a friend. His friend notices, however, that the private shows no concern—he is not resentful or upset at having his plans spoiled, nor does he give evidence of thinking that the commander has forgotten his promise and ought to be reminded. Nor does he have the grim appearance of one who is resigned. Rather, he almost appears not to understand his situation. The surprised friend asks, "Well, aren't you going to do anything about it? You certainly have a legitimate gripe—or if you think the old man has forgotten his promise why don't you go and remind him?"

Now the private looks surprised. "Legitimate gripe? About what? Of course he hasn't forgotten his promise. I'll have my pass."

"Oh, you think that your name being on the guard roster for the weekend is a mistake. Well, you'd better get it straightened out."

"No, there's no mistake. I'm on guard duty all right."

"Well, then, who've you decided to ask to take your place? Not me, I've got a pass, too."

"Nobody's going to take my place. I'm going to stand guard myself."

"What do you mean, you're going to stand guard yourself? You said you were going on pass!"

There is no need to continue this dialogue. The similarity to

Abraham's situation should now be apparent: just as Abraham believed that God's promise to him would be fulfilled, while at the same time intending to obey God's command, so the private believes that his commander's promise to him will be fulfilled, while at the same time intending to obey his command. About either case we might shake our heads and exclaim, "That's a paradox!" And of either paradox we might also be inclined to say that the paradox is "real."

Concerning the private's situation, one can see what the paradox is and also its "realness." First, the paradox is that, unaccountably, the private both believes that a promise will be fulfilled, the fulfillment of which precludes the possibility of obeying the command, and also intends to obey a command the obeying of which precludes the possibility of the promise's being fulfilled. The realness of the paradox is that this preclusion is, as we shall now put it, absolute. If the promise is fulfilled then the command cannot be obeyed; and if the command is obeyed then the promise cannot be fulfilled.

This sort of "real" paradox is to be distinguished from apparent paradoxes, of which the following argument is an example:

> He who is most hungry eats most. He who eats least is most hungry. Therefore, he who eats least eats most.[12]

This argument paradoxically proves true what appears to be a self-contradiction. It is a syllogism in the first figure, mood AAA, and thus is valid. And yet the conclusion appears to be self-contradictory. Prima facie the argument is paradoxical, and one might explain one's calling it paradoxical by saying, "A valid argument cannot have a self-contradictory conclusion, and yet here, it seems, we have one that does." The prima facie paradoxicalness of the syllogism is removed, however, when one points out that the major premise means "He who is most hungry *will eat most*" and that the minor premise means "He who *has eaten least* is most hungry." Making these changes in the verb phrases of the conclusion as well as of the premises then eliminates the paradoxicalness of the argument, for the conclusion now reads "He who has eaten least will eat most." The paradox is thus only apparent and not real. In contrast, the paradox in the case of the private has no such resolution. One cannot eliminate it by rephrasing the statement of the situation.

Let us examine the private's case a little more closely to see what is involved in its containing a real paradox. The private both believes that the promise will be fulfilled and intends to obey the command. Now, as was brought out in the presentation of this case, the private intends to obey the command himself. He is not thinking of getting someone else to obey it for him so that while he is in town dancing with the USO girls, his friend is trudging along a dark fenceline with an M1 rifle on his shoulder. Rather, what the private believes and intends must be taken to involve that it might come about that while he is in town dancing with the USO girls he is also walking his post along fenceline, that is, that one person might be in two places at once.

The immediate reaction of course is "But one person can't be in two different places at once!" And this is a way of saying that the meaning of the expression "one person" is such that it *makes no sense* to say of one person that he was in two different places at once. This may be seen if we consider what we call "counting persons." Consider this case. The commanding officer of Company B wishes to know how many of his men are on pass for the evening. He does not have the pass book with him and so asks one of his company officers to go to the USO club and another to look in at the pool hall next to the club, these being the only places outside the camp where his men take their ease. The company officers make their investigations. The first officer reports that he counted only one man from Company B at the USO club; the second officer likewise reports that he counted but one at the pool hall. The commanding officer hesitates: "But you may have counted one person twice. What time was it when you made your counts?" And what will settle it for the commander that his officers have not counted one person twice is this: that they made their counts at the same time. What is *counted* as "one person," then, is not something that can, like poverty, be in more than one place at the same time. We do not call "one person" that of which it makes sense to suggest that it is in two places at the same time.

Let us now return to the case of the private. We said of this case that if the promise is fulfilled then the command cannot be obeyed and if the command is obeyed then the promise cannot be fulfilled. We can now see why. For the promise and the command in conjunction *rule out* precisely what they *require*: they require the possibility of calling the receiver of the pass and the obeyer of the command "one person," since the person who is to receive the pass is the person who is to obey the command; and yet they rule this out as a possibility, since we do not call "one person" that of which it makes sense to suggest that it is in two places at once. Thus, the promise and the command in conjunction make no sense.

If the promise and the command in conjunction are nonsense, the paradox is that the private should believe the promise will be fulfilled and should also intend to obey the command. "How can he!" we want to exclaim. "For together the promise and the command are nonsense!" We might at this point go on to discuss the question whether it makes sense to say that one believes or intends what is nonsense. But for our purpose it is enough to have pointed out that the promise and command in conjunction are nonsense and that the paradox is that the private both believes that the promise will be fulfilled and also intends to obey the command.

Let us now return to Abraham and ask, "Is his case like that of the private? Are we to say that here too the promise and the command in conjunction are nonsense and that the paradox is that Abraham believes that the promise will be fulfilled and also intends to obey the command?" First, are the promise and the command in conjunction nonsense? One might wish to say so, for if the promise is that through Isaac Abraham's seed should be multiplied as the stars of the heaven and the command is that Isaac should be sacrificed, then the promise and command in conjunction involve that a dead boy should grow to manhood, marry, and father children. And as in the private's case we said, "One person can't be in two different places at once" in order to point out that the promise and the command in conjunction make no sense, so in the case of Abraham we might wish to say, "A dead boy cannot grow up, marry, and father children," in order to point out that here too the promise and the command in conjunction make no sense. In this latter case we might go on to explain that the very meaning of the word "dead" is "a ceasing of life processes—growth, and so forth." And so about a dead person it makes no sense to ask how much he has grown in the last six months, to inquire whether he has met a nice girl yet, to wonder whether he has a family yet, and so on. And this is true; it does make no sense.

But there is a mistake in all this. The mistake is in thinking that the promise and the command in conjunction involve the nonsense that a dead boy should grow to manhood, marry, and father children. They involve, rather, that Abraham's living son grow to manhood, marry, and father children. And how is this to be accomplished? (Abraham never asked this question. But we who want to get the logic of the situation straight must ask it.) The answer is supplied by Kierkegaard on pages 46–47 of *Fear and Trembling*: "Let us go further. We let Isaac be really sacrificed. Abraham believed. He did not believe that some day he would be blessed in the beyond, but that he would be happy here in the world. God . . . could recall to life him who had been sacrificed."[13]

This passage shows that Kierkegaard did not regard Abraham

as one who was being asked to "believe" the logically impossible or the nonsensical, whatever it might mean to say of one that he believes such. There is, rather, something that we should all call fulfillment of the promise, even though the command has been obeyed. (Contrast the case of the private: there is nothing we should call fulfillment of the promise if the command is obeyed.)

But then what is Kierkegaard calling paradoxical in the case of Abraham? Is it not just what Abraham did? Is it not his believing that the promise would yet be fulfilled even while he obeyed a command the obeying of which rendered fulfillment of the promise impossible—*except by a miracle?* Is this not the "enormous paradox which is the substance of Abraham's life"? Is this not what Johannes de silentio cannot understand—cannot understand because it is absurd? There is little difficulty in imagining the Abraham story (not, at least, with Kierkegaard's help), but can we imagine doing what Abraham did, the while expecting what Abraham expected? But this point is best brought home by Kierkegaard himself.

At the beginning of section III of this chapter I asked the question: does the paradox of religiousness *B*, as it is exemplified in the case of Abraham, involve a logical contradiction or impossibility? If what I went on to say is correct, then we can say that, *in the case of Abraham*, the paradox does not involve a logical contradiction or impossibility. We might, however, still have doubts about the God-man paradox, which for Kierkegaard is peculiar to Christianity. For though one might argue that since both the religion of Abraham and Christianity are instances of religiousness *B*, the paradoxical religion, and the paradox in Abraham's case involves no logical impossibility, then the paradox in the case of Christianity involves no logical impossibility—the argument is very weak. I do not wish to propound it. I think, however, that its conclusion is correct. Would Kierkegaard saw off the limb he is sitting on?

4 / The Absolute Paradox: The God-Man

IN an essay that appeared in *Religious Studies*, G. G. O'Collins concludes with a question that in his view states "the classic problem of Christology": "What is the ontological connection between the Logos and the human existence of Jesus of Nazareth?"[1] C. J. F. Williams, in a later issue of the same journal, poses the question, "What *sort* of union is a hypostatic union?"[2] In the literature grown up around Kierkegaard's pronouncements on the notion of the God-man, the following question is discussed: Did Kierkegaard mean to say that the very notion of the God-man is incoherent? Some hold that he did, some that he did not. Yet, however important it is to establish what Kierkegaard himself held concerning this question, there is the far more important question for Christian doctrine of whether the notion of the God-man *is* incoherent.

This chapter is intended as a contribution toward the settling of these and some related difficulties. Section I presents two plausible reactions to Kierkegaard's rather obscure pronouncements on the God-man. The first reaction is, I think, the correct one concerning the question of his intention; the second, though obviously not correct, is the more interesting, because it allows us to get hold of the question of incoherence or self-contradictoriness in a manageable form by allowing us, at the beginning, to focus on but a few of the many "contrary things," as Aquinas called them—those pairs of predicates that characterize, and render perplexing, the idea of the God-man. In effect, the pairs being considered in section I are these: temporal and eternal, and created and uncreated. Section II carries the question forward by placing it in the setting of the confrontation between heresy and orthodoxy in the Early Church. Section III deals with what I call the general form of the charge of self-contradiction. Section IV is concerned with Williams's question "What sort of union is a hypostatic union?" Section V deals with what I refer to as the particular form of the charge of self-contradiction, and VI concerns the dispute between Nestorianism and orthodoxy over the proper completion of the doctrinal sentence that begins "The Son of God assumed. . . ." O'Collins's question, "What is the ontological connection between the Logos and the human existence of Jesus of Nazareth?" I do not explicitly treat, but I hope that my discussion of closely related difficulties will shed some light on the problem it addresses.

I

I turn now to Kierkegaard's absolute paradox, the paradox of the God-man. The *Concluding Unscientific Postscript* contains several versions of it. One of them is this: "That God has existed in human form, has been born, grown up, and so forth." In addition to calling this "the absolute paradox," Kierkegaard characterizes it (in another version) as "the absurd" and (in apparently any of its versions) as "the unintelligible." He also says that the paradox, the absurd, involves a contradiction and that "it is this contradiction which constitutes the absurd" and "is a breach with all thinking."

But Kierkegaard also characterizes the idea of the God-man in ways that are at least seemingly inconsistent with those just recited. For although it is "the absurd" and "the unintelligible," it is also sometimes "the improbable" (*Postscript*, p. 209),[3] "the most improbable of things" (*Philosophical Fragments*, p. 42), and "the Miracle" (ibid.); and although it involves a contradiction and is a breach with all thinking, it is nevertheless not "nonsense" (*Postscript*, p. 504). How, one is disposed to ask, could something which is absurd and unintelligible also be merely "the improbable"? And how could something involve contradiction and be a breach with all thinking, and yet not be nonsense?

There are no doubt several possible reactions to these two at least seemingly inconsistent ways of characterizing the idea of the God-man. Immediately following are two such reactions. The first is this.

"When Kierkegaard uses such terms as 'contradiction' and 'unintelligible' to characterize the idea of the God-man, he is either using them in some nonliteral or loose sense or is somehow confused. For if he must be read as saying that the idea of the God-man involves a *logical* contradiction or that it is *literally* unintelligible, then he is portraying the Christian as a 'believer' of plain nonsense. And this is at odds not merely with his remark in the *Postscript* (p. 504) that 'nonsense . . . [the Christian] cannot believe against the understanding, for precisely the understanding will discern that it is nonsense and will prevent him from believing it,' but is also at odds with the whole intention of his Christian authorship. On the other hand, his characterization of the idea of the God-man as 'the improbable,' 'the most improbable of things,' and 'the Miracle' is quite in accord with the Christian intention of his work. For near the center of this intention is his desire to keep Christianity from being 'transformed from an existence communication into a metaphysical doctrine appropriate to professors'; to keep God's appearance in history from being represented as a phenomenon to be so 'interpenetrated' with 'speculative thought' that it comes to be seen as something inevitable in world history and somehow provable in speculative thought. It was, then, to prevent or at least to combat this 'transformation,' this misrepresentation, that Kierkegaard characterized God's appearance in history, the idea of the God-man, as 'the improbable,' 'the most improbable of things,' and 'the Miracle.' So far from being demonstrably inevitable in the movement of history, God's appearance, he was saying, was the most improbable of things—*the* Miracle, whose occurrence was and will always be simply outside the realm of any sort of human calculation. But of course Kierkegaard did not mean also to be saying that the description of this miracle, the idea of the God-man, contains a *contradiction* in the logicians' sense of that word or is literally *unintelligible*, for this would be tantamount to saying, not that the occurrence of the miracle is outside the realm of human calculation, but that no occurrence, miraculous or natural, could answer to the so-called description, since the 'description' is no more than a meaningless jumble of words. *This* Kierkegaard did not mean to say—and if in certain places his language forces this interpretation on his reader it must be put down to a regrettable but only momentary confusion in his thought. His larger meaning is clear."

This, then, is the first reaction to Kierkegaard's apparently inconsistent ways of characterizing the idea of the God-man. The second reaction will be presented in the form of a reply to the first.

"You say that if in certain places Kierkegaard's language forces us to read him as saying (at these places) that the God-man idea is no more than a meaningless jumble of words, this must be put down to a regrettable but only momentary confusion in his thought. I disagree. If his characterization of the idea of the God-man by the words 'contradiction,' 'unintelligible,' 'absurd,' and so on must be understood in a literal fashion (and whether it must or not I do not wish to argue), then what Kierkegaard is saying here is by no means regrettable. For these words of his—

and whether they were written inadvertently in confusion or intentionally in moments of great clarity is here a question that need not concern us—these *words* of his express the *true* character of the idea of the God-man. The idea *is* absurd; it *does* involve contradiction; it *is* a breach with all thinking; it *is* unintelligible. The 'idea' of the God-man is, in short, not an *idea* at all, but a meaningless jumble of words. And credit is due, if not to Kierkegaard, then to Kierkegaard's language for having indicated this.

"But Kierkegaard does more than merely *point* to the unintelligibility by employing such words as 'contradiction,' 'unintelligible,' and so on. By the very language in which he often couches the idea, he also *displays* its unintelligibility. For though he sometimes expresses the idea as God's having come into being and God's having existed in human form, which expressions tend to conceal the unintelligibility, he more often expresses the idea in terms of eternality and temporality; and when he expresses it in these terms, the unintelligibility is evident. One such expression is this: 'that that which in accordance with its nature is eternal comes into existence in time, is born, grows up, and dies.' The idea, then, whose unintelligibility Kierkegaard has so well characterized and displayed is the idea that God, *who is eternal*, should be born, grow up, and die—that one who, as Saint Paul puts it, 'existed before creation began,' should be born, that is, should *begin to exist*, in the days of Herod. What is more clearly contradictory, what more clearly unintelligible than the notion that someone who *began* to exist at a certain date, nevertheless existed *before* that date and indeed 'existed before creation began'? This notion obviously involves the notion that someone both *did* and *did not* exist at a certain time, for example, the time of King David or the time of Abraham. That is the contradiction, the piece of unintelligibility, which Kierkegaard characterized and displayed so clearly.

"Now it may be thought that the idea of the God-man thus characterized and displayed is a distortion of Scripture. It is not.

Consider, for example, a passage (John 17:5) in which Jesus prays to the Father as follows: 'Now, Father, honour me in your own presence with the glory that I knew with you before the world was made.' Another translation has the same passage as follows: 'And now, O Father, glorify thou me with thine own self with the glory which I had with thee before the world was.' How is the meaning of this utterance to be understood otherwise than as involving the implication that Jesus existed before the world was made? And other passages have the same implication. There is John 17:24, where Jesus says in prayer: 'Father, I will that they also, whom thou hast given me, be with me where I am; that they may behold my glory, which thou hast given me: for thou lovedst me before the foundation of the world.' The last clause surely involves the same implication. And so must, though perhaps less obviously, the passages in which Jesus refers to himself as having come down from heaven (John 3:13 and cf. John 3:31), as having been sent by God (John 5:36; 6:29; 8:42), and as teaching that which he has heard of, seen with, and learned of God (John 8:23, 26, 28, 38, 40). Consider, also, John 8:56–58, in which Jesus speaks to the Jews: 'Your father Abraham rejoiced to see my day: and he saw it, and was glad. Then said the Jews unto him, Thou art not yet fifty years old, and hast thou seen Abraham? Jesus said unto them, Verily, verily, I say unto you, Before Abraham was, I am.' The implication here is that Jesus, although 'not yet fifty years old' existed during and before the lifetime of Abraham.

"In addition to these passages, which report Jesus' own words, there are the following. 'Christ existed before creation began' (Col. 1:15); speaking of Melchisedec, a priest mentioned in Genesis 14, the writer of Hebrews says (7:3): 'He was not born nor did he die, but, being like the Son of God, is a perpetual priest,' the implication being that the Son of God was not born; 'you have known him [Christ] who has always existed' (I John 2:13); 'But this man [Jesus], because he continueth ever, hath an unchangeable priesthood" (Heb. 7:24); the author of Hebrews writes that the Father addressed his Son as follows: 'And, Thou, Lord, in the beginning hast laid the foundation of the earth; and the heavens are the works of thine hands' (1:10), the implication again being that the Son existed before creation began; 'for it was through him that everything was made' (Col. 1:16).

"These passages taken together imply that Jesus Christ existed before the days of Herod, during and before the time of Abraham, and even before the world was made. And yet there are also scriptural passages which state that Jesus Christ was *born* in the days of Herod—and so of course did not exist before that time. There is, for example, Luke 2:11: 'This very day, in David's town, a Saviour has been born for you. He is Christ, the Lord.' And there is Matthew 2:1: 'Jesus was born in Bethlehem, in Judaea, in the days when Herod was king of the province.'

"From all these passages it is clear that the idea of the God-man as Kierkegaard displays and characterizes it, is not a distortion of Scripture. For it is according to Scripture that Jesus Christ was born in the days of Herod and also that he existed before the days of Herod: that he both did and did not exist before the days of Herod. It is this scriptural 'idea' that Kierkegaard (or at least his language) correctly displays and characterizes as absurd, contradictory, and unintelligible—or, as you yourself put it earlier, as no more than a meaningless jumble of words. Nor is this display and characterization (as you thought) regrettable, for it is correct. The Christian is in truth a 'believer' in plain nonsense."

This second reaction is correct in this: that it is according to Scripture that Jesus Christ was born in the days of Herod and also that he existed before the days of Herod. One may, however, wish to object that the inference drawn from this is unwarranted, the inference, namely, that Jesus both did and did not exist before the days of Herod. Specifically, one may wish to deny that from the texts that tell us that Jesus was born in the days of Herod it can be inferred that he did not exist before that time. For (the reasoning may go), since according to Scripture Jesus "was come from

God," was "with God" in the beginning, it must be supposed that the phrase "was born" as applied to him has a sense different from the one it has when applied to us: that when it is said that I was born at a certain time what is meant is that I came to exist at that time, but that when it is said that Jesus was born at a certain time it is *not* meant that he came to exist at that time. Thus (the objection continues) it is a mistake to infer from the texts telling us that Jesus was born in the days of Herod that he did not exist until that time; and so it is also a mistake to infer from the scriptural passages cited in the second reaction that Jesus both did and did not exist before the days of Herod. What *can* be inferred or got from those passages is this: that Jesus was born in the days of Herod (there being no implication that he did not exist before that time) and also that he existed before that time. There is, then, contrary to the contention in the second reaction, nothing to be called a contradiction here.

The following reply may be made to this objection. The substance of the objection is contained in the contention that "was born" is not univocal in its application to Jesus and its application to (say) oneself: "that when it is said that I was born at a certain time what is meant is that I came to exist at that time, but that when it is said that Jesus was born at a certain time it is *not* meant that he came to exist at that time." But this is to say, for example, that the sentence "But he was not *born* until the reign of Caesar Augustus" can properly be used as a means of rejecting questions concerning the whereabouts and activities during (say) the time of Julius Caesar of someone of Jesus' generation, for example of John the Baptist, but that this same sentence applied to Jesus himself *cannot* be so used. But surely the sentence can be used in this way, would be understood as a denial of the assumption of existence in the time of Julius Caesar, in *both* cases. Again, to object that the phrase "was born" as applied to Jesus has a sense different from the ordinary is to suggest that Jesus was not a "true man" (for one is suggesting that he was not "truly born"). It is to make a step in the construction of (in Kierkegaard's phrase) "a fantastic figure of Christ," the heresy of Docetism. It is, then, quite right to infer or get from the scriptural passages cited in the second reaction the idea that Jesus was born in the days of Herod (this meaning that he came to exist at that time, with, of course, the implication that he did not exist before that time)[4] and also that he existed before that time. Thus the contention of the second reaction is correct that it is according to Scripture that Jesus Christ both did and did not exist before the days of Herod.[5]

II

According to Scripture, Jesus Christ both did and did not exist before the days of Herod. But is it, then, correct to characterize this scriptural idea as self-contradictory and the Christian as a "believer" in plain nonsense? Doing so seems unavoidable. What could be more obviously self-contradictory, what plainer nonsense, than that Christ both did and did not exist before the days of Herod?

The difficulty is as old as Christianity and is one that has been felt for a long time. The history of heresy in the Early Church, as C. J. F. Williams has suggested, may almost be read as several attempts to avoid the charge of self-contradiction.[6] The heresy of Ebionism denies Christ's Godhead, or to retain the terms we have thus far used, it denies that Christ existed before the days of Herod. Docetism, on the other hand, denies Christ's manhood, or, again to use our former terms, denies that he did not exist before the days of Herod. Nestorianism denies neither that Christ did exist before the days of Herod nor that he did not. Instead it holds that there are two persons in Christ, a divine person and a human person, and that it is the divine person that existed before the days of Herod and the human person that did not.

Williams also contends that the orthodox formulas (for example, the Definition of Chalcedon) "serve to rule out the brash solutions offered by the heresiarchs," and "do little themselves except to sharpen the edges of the problem."[7] Against Ebionism orthodoxy maintains that Christ was "truly God," or, again using our original terms, that he existed before the days of Herod. Against Docetism orthodoxy maintains that Christ was "truly man," that he did not exist before the days of Herod. Against Nestorianism orthodoxy maintains that what is said both to have existed and to have not existed before the days of Herod is one person, not two. Thus against these heresies, orthodoxy, Williams would claim, seems to do little more than reassert the sort of scriptural idea we have instanced in this: that Jesus Christ (who is just one person) both did and did not exist before the days of Herod. But to reassert an idea alleged to be self-contradictory is not to provide a reason to withdraw the allegation. And so orthodoxy seems to offer no satisfactory solution.

But we must not sell orthodoxy short here. There may be at least the germ of a solution in the orthodox formula for the hypostatic union: one person existing in two natures. In this formula is suggested the possibility of responding to the charge of self-contradiction in the following way: "According to Scripture, Christ both did and did not exist before the days of Herod. But this scriptural claim is not self-contradictory. For what is being claimed is that Christ *as God* existed before the days of Herod and that Christ *as a man* did not exist before the days of Herod."[8]

This response, however, may be seen as mere sand throwing. For one may say: "To say that Christ as God existed before the days of Herod and that Christ as a man did not exist before the days of Herod is only to say that Christ is one of whom it may be said (among other things characterizing him as God or the Son of God) that he existed before the days of Herod; and that Christ is one of whom it may be said (among other things characterizing him as a man) that he did *not* exist before the days of Herod. But even if there may be said of him other things characterizing him as God and still others as a man, the self-contradiction remains.

And this will be so regardless of what the two sets of characterizations—as God and as a man—are supposed to contain. For whatever they contain, they *also* contain the claim that Christ existed before the days of Herod and the claim that he did not. The orthodox attempt to evade the charge of self-contradiction is thus no better than the following: Suppose I say that I have drawn a plane figure on a piece of paper. I 'describe' it as having right angles and also as not having right angles. To the charge that my 'description' is self-contradictory, I say: 'Well, but you see, the figure as a square has right angles and the figure as a circle does not have right angles.' Clearly, if I said this, I would merely be throwing sand or making a poor joke. My attempt to evade the charge comes to this: the supposed figure is one of which it may be said (among other things characterizing it as a square) that it has right angles; and the supposed figure is one of which it may be said (among other things characterizing it as a circle) that it does not have right angles. Even without questioning the additional things characterizing it, on the one hand, as a square and, on the other, as a circle, we can see that the charge of self-contradiction is justified. For what is said *contains* both the claim that the supposed figure has right angles and the claim that it does not. The orthodox attempt to evade the charge of self-contradiction succeeds no better than this one."

III

We have just seen how the orthodox attempt to avoid the charge of self-contradiction may be taken as mere sand throwing. The orthodox formula "Christ as God existed, etc., and Christ as a man did not exist, etc." looks similar—and for orthodoxy uncomfortably similar—to "the figure as a square has right angles and the figure as a circle does not have right angles." But if understood in the light of a different analogy, the orthodox attempt may be seen as something better than sand throwing.

The analogy I have in mind is with the now familiar figure of the duck-rabbit (see Wittgenstein's *Philosophical Investigations*, p. 194). The figure will be helpful in several ways. First, to begin with what is easiest to dispose of, suppose the charge of self-contradiction takes the following general form.

"Consider statements of the form '*X* as *A* is *N*, and *X* as *B* is not *N*' where the following five conditions are met:

(1) What replaces *X* in both its occurrences has the same meaning or reference (will have the same explanation).

(2) What replaces *N* in both its occurrences has the same meaning (will have the same explanation).

(3) *A* and *B* each stand proxy for a set of predicables.

(4) '*X* as *A*' predicates set *A* of *X*; likewise, '*X* as *B*' predicates set *B* of *X*.

(5) '*X* as *A* is *N*' indicates that *N* is a member of set *A*; likewise, '*X* as *B* is not *N*' indicates that 'not *N*' is a member of set *B*.

"In statements of the form in question that meet these five conditions, it will be seen that as a member of the set for which *A* stands proxy *N* is predicated of *X*, but that as a member of the set for which *B* stands proxy 'not *N*' is also predicated of *X*. By being members of their respective sets, both *N* and 'not *N*' are predicated of *X*. Therefore, statements having the form and analysis just set forth are self-contradictory.

"Apparent counterexamples such as 'Simmias as compared with Socrates is tall, but Simmias as compared with Phaedo is not tall' do not meet condition 5 of the analysis. Moreover, it is doubtful that they meet conditions 3 and 4. Allowing, however, that the latter two conditions are met—that is, that 'compared with Socrates' and 'compared with Phaedo' each designate a set of predicables and that 'Simmias as compared with Socrates' and 'Simmias as compared with Phaedo' each predicate their own set of Simmias—condition 5 is plainly not met. For it is clear that

'Simmias as compared with Socrates is tall' cannot be taken to indicate that 'tall' is part of the package of predicables designated by 'compared with Socrates' and gets predicated of Simmias by being part of that package. If this were so, then wherever the *package* was 'truly predicated,' 'tall' would be truly predicated as well. But it is clear that 'tall' is not truly predicated in every case where 'compared with Socrates' is. For example, in 'General Tom Thumb as compared with Socrates is tall' the package 'compared with Socrates' is 'truly predicated' but 'tall' is not. Thus, because condition 5 is not met, the Socrates statement is not a true counterexample.

"Condition 5, as well as the other conditions, *is* met, however, by the Christological statement we are concerned with: namely, 'Christ as God existed before the days of Herod and Christ as a man did not exist before the days of Herod.' Here 'God' and 'a man' each designate a set of predicables (condition 3 is met); 'Christ as God' and 'Christ as a man' each predicate their own set of Christ (condition 4 is met); 'Christ as God existed before, etc.' indicates that 'existed before, etc.' is a member of the set 'God' and 'Christ as a man did not exist before, etc.' indicates that 'did not exist before, etc.' is a member of the set 'a man' (condition 5 is met). Thus both 'existed before, etc.' and 'did not exist before, etc.,' by being members of their respective packages of predicables, get predicated of Christ. The result here, as in the case of every other statement of the same form and analysis, is self-contradiction."

To this general form of the charge of self-contradiction, orthodoxy can respond by producing an example of the required form, one that meets the five conditions at least as well and clearly as the Christological statement does but is nevertheless not self-contradictory. Orthodoxy's procedure here will strongly suggest that despite all appearances to the contrary the Christological statement really does not meet the five conditions. The question whether or not it does meet them, however, need not be pursued. For if it does not meet them, the general form of the charge has no plausibility whatever; and if it does meet them, as it seems to, orthodoxy's counterexample still shows that the charge's fundamental claim—that all statements that have the form and analysis set forth are self-contradictory—is false.

Orthodoxy's response to the charge can go as follows: "I will not deny that *most* statements of the sort being considered are self-contradictory. Nevertheless, not all of them are. By producing a counterexample, I will show that the major premise—namely, 'Any and all statements having the form and analysis set forth are self-contradictory'—from which the charge against the Christological statement is derived is false and the argument therefore unsound. The counterexample is a remark made as part of the answer to a riddle: 'What has long, pointed ears, but doesn't have long, pointed ears?' Answer: 'The duck-rabbit. As a rabbit the figure has long, pointed ears, but as a duck, it does not.' The second sentence of this answer clearly is of the form in question. (The slight syntactical and grammatical departure from the form can hardly be thought to matter.) The statement also meets our five conditions at least as well and clearly as the Christological statement. (1) What replaces *X* in both its occurrences—namely, 'the figure' and 'it'—has the same reference and would be explained in the same way, should an explanation be required. (2) What replaces *N* in both its occurrences—namely, 'has (or, does have) long, pointed ears'—means the same in both places (would have the same explanation). (3) 'A rabbit' and 'a duck' each designate a set of predicables. (4) 'The figure as a rabbit' and 'the figure as a duck' each predicate their own set of the figure. (5) 'The figure as a rabbit has long, pointed ears' indicates that 'has long, etc.' is a member of the set 'a rabbit' and 'the figure as a duck does not have long, pointed ears' indicates that 'does not have long, etc.' is a member of the set 'a duck.' But even though the remark from the answer to the riddle has the form in question and meets conditions 1–5 as well and clearly as the Christological statement does, it is clearly not self-contradictory. That is, its right hand does not take back what its left hand gives, unlike the poor joke concerning the 'square circle': 'The figure as a square has right angles; the figure as a circle does not have right angles.'" Thus the general form of the charge of self-contradiction against the orthodox claim fails.[9]

IV

Williams asks, "What *sort* of union is a hypostatic union?" He goes on to say that orthodoxy does not contain a satisfactory answer to this question. Ian Ramsey, as though in response to Williams, says that the word "hypostasis" is "resistant to any and all modelling," that "it is quite impossible (*logically* impossible) to produce a model for it."[10] What Ramsey appears to mean by this is that if one seeks a model for the orthodox claim that Christ is one person who is both truly God and truly a man, one will inevitably find oneself with something that misrepresents this claim in one of two important ways. One's model will misrepresent Christ as consisting of two persons, as for example the model of a man and a woman united in marriage would do. Or, to err in the other direction, one's model will represent Christ as not being truly God and truly a man, but as being partly God and partly a man, as the model of a centaur (partly man and partly horse) would do.[11] There is and can be, Ramsey is saying, no model which does not misrepresent the orthodox claim—and in particular none which can steer us safely between the rock of Nestorianism (the man and wife model) and the whirlpool of Eutychianism (the centaur model). Thus, read as a response to Williams's question "What *sort* of union is a hypostatic union?" Ramsey's words are a rejection of it. Ramsey implies that the hypostatic union is not a *sort* of union at all. For if it were, then surely it could be modeled—*something* could be like it in the relevant ways, *something* spoken of in relevantly similar ways, something serve as the focus of a grammatical analogy.

The figure of the duck-rabbit will, I think, serve. The orthodox claim is that Christ is one person who is both truly God and truly a man. The duck-rabbit is one figure that is both "truly" a duck and "truly" a rabbit. If we understand the orthodox claim on the model of the duck-rabbit figure, do we avoid the rock of Nestorianism? Suppose the Nestorian notion of two persons to have been arrived at in the following way: Suppose Nestorius, thinking about the matter in quite general terms, to have asked himself, "How can one thing (for example, a shoe, or a ship, or a cabbage) be *two* things (that is, have two natures)? That is, how can a cabbage, for instance, be both a cabbage and, say, a ship? It cannot, of course. Each thing has but one nature. That is, it is a shoe, *or* a ship, *or* a cabbage. So if in Christ there are two natures, there have to be *two* things, persons in this case." If this is roughly the way in which the notion of two persons in Christ was developed, then it is clear that in modeling the orthodox claim on the figure of the duck-rabbit we avoid the rock of Nestorianism. For there are here not *two* figures, one a duck, the other a rabbit, juxtaposed (whether drawn with one continuous line or not), or one superimposed upon the other. There is but one figure such that if one traces with one's finger the outline of the duck one is perforce tracing that of the rabbit: one disposition of a single segment of line forms both the duck and the rabbit. Thus, the one thing (the duck-rabbit figure) is two things (the figure of a duck and also the figure of a rabbit). And Nestorius, at least as we have represented him, is seen to be the victim of a one-sided diet of examples.[12]

But if we avoid the rock of Nestorianism, have we fallen into the whirlpool of Eutychianism? I think not. For the figure is not partly duck and partly rabbit, having, say, a rabbit's ears and a duck's bill, as a centaur has a man's head, arms and torso and a horse's body and legs. It is at once "truly" a duck and "truly" a rabbit. (Nor, to remark on another form of Eutychianism, does one deny that it is either a duck or a rabbit by pointing out that it is a duck-rabbit. For it would not be a duck-rabbit unless it was *also* identifiably a duck, and *also* identifiably a rabbit. The term "duck-rabbit" does not designate, to employ the theological term, a third "nature" in which the duck and the rabbit have somehow been swallowed up—as, perhaps, the vowel sounds *ah* and *ee* are swallowed up in the sound *eye* if they are produced together rapidly enough in the order *ah-ee*. In the "union" of duck and rabbit, the two maintain their identities. They are, to use a term from the Definition of Chalcedon, "without confusion.")

Thus, the duck-rabbit figure appears to be a model of the sort that Ramsey claims it is logically impossible to produce, a model of the hypostatic union which conducts us safely between the rock of Nestorianism and the whirlpool of Eutychianism. And to Williams's question "What *sort* of union is a hypostatic union?" (understood as a request for a safe route between these two perils), we have provided a reply: "It is the sort exhibited by the duck-rabbit figure."

V

In section III of this chapter we considered a general form of the charge of self-contradiction against the claim: "Christ as God existed before the days of Herod, and Christ as a man did not exist before the days of Herod." We saw that the charge in its general form fails. We must now consider it in a more particular and troublesome form.

Thus: "It is all very well to say that the charge in its general form fails. The counterexample about the duck-rabbit figure shows that it is wrong to say that all claims of the form 'X as A is N, and X as *B* is not *N*,' where there is appropriate univocalness among the terms, are self-contradictory. But not even the duck-rabbit figure can show that when *N* stands for a temporal predicate of the sort 'existed before time *T*' (and 'existed before the days of Herod' is of this sort), the charge of self-contradiction fails. In fact, consideration of this figure can provide us a reason for thinking the charge correct. Suppose I tell you that I have just drawn a duck-rabbit figure on a sheet of paper. After a fifteen-second interval I ring a bell. After another fifteen-second interval I make this 'claim': 'As a duck, it existed before the bell rang; but as a rabbit it did not exist before the bell rang.' Clearly this 'claim' involves a self-contradiction. For what I have 'claimed' is that the duck-rabbit figure I say I have drawn both did and did not exist before the bell rang, and neither the two occurrences of the pronoun 'it' (standing, it should be noticed, in both places for the phrase 'the duck-rabbit figure') nor the phrases 'as a duck' and 'as a rabbit' should stand in the way of one's seeing this. If as a duck the duck-rabbit figure existed before the bell rang, then, *being a duck-rabbit figure*, as a rabbit, too, it existed before the bell rang. Or, if as a rabbit the duck-rabbit figure did not exist before the bell rang, then, *being a duck-rabbit figure*, as a duck, too, it did not exist before the bell rang. The duck-rabbit figure *could* not as a duck exist before the bell rang while as a rabbit not do so. Thus the duck-rabbit figure does not provide a counterexample whereby the charge of self-contradiction is shown to fail against claims of the form '*X* as A is *N*, and *X* as *B* is not *N*' (where *N* stands for a predicate of the sort 'existed before time *T*'). Indeed, since my 'claim' about the duck-rabbit figure is of this form and since this 'claim' has been shown to be self-contradictory, the figure, so far from yielding a reason to think that the charge fails, actually provides reason for thinking that it succeeds against any claim of the form in question, including the claim 'Christ as God existed before the days of Herod and as a man did not.' To add spice to the pot, this failure is, it seems, all the more serious in view of the heavy reliance you have so far placed [in sections III and IV of this chapter] on the figure as the focus of a grammatical analogy. For the (at least apparent) grammatical similarities so far pointed out generate a momentum such that on coming to consider *this* detail, this temporal feature, in the grammar of 'Christ' and finding its counterpart in the grammar of 'duck-rabbit' to involve self-contradiction, you seem to be faced with a serious dilemma: either you must think that the help you have so far seemed to get from the duck-rabbit figure (in dealing with the general form of the charge of self-contradiction and with the claim that a model of the hypostatic union is logically impossible to produce) is quite spurious and your reliance on it a mistake from the outset, or you must think that you were right to rely on the figure and now must grimly accept what it shows you—namely, that just as: 'The duck-rabbit figure as a duck existed before the bell rang and as a rabbit did not' involves self-contradiction, so also: 'Christ as God existed before the days of Herod and as a man did not' involves a self-contradition. I am saying: you must, it seems, either drop the duck-rabbit figure and start over from the very beginning, or admit that the claim about Christ is self-contradictory."

Now neither of these alternatives need be accepted. One need not say that the claim about Christ is self-contradictory; nor need one repudiate the duck-rabbit figure. What is required is not a repudiation, but a complication of it. And that a complication is required at this point in no way abrogates the usefulness of its simpler version in dealing with the difficulties on which in the foregoing pages we have brought it to bear. For our complicated version of the figure, in addition to enabling us to deal with the charge of self-contradiction presently under consideration, would have been helpful in dealing with those difficulties in precisely the *same* ways as the simpler version was.

The complicated version of the duck-rabbit figure that will serve us here is a cinematic duck-rabbit. Here, then, is the scenario for a simple animated cartoon.

The film opens showing only the figure of a rabbit's head. After five minutes, during which time there is no movement or change, a tone sounds while the head undergoes an alteration: among other, less easily noticeable changes, a drooping ear straightens, and the rabbit's head, without losing even momentarily the character of a rabbit's head, becomes the figure of a duck-rabbit. Three minutes more elapse, during which time there is again no change. Finis.

Looking now to the cinematic duck-rabbit for assistance, we can take a short way with the charge under consideration. We can respond: There is no more reason here to think that the claim "Christ as God existed before the days of Herod, but as a man did not" involves a self-contradiction than there is to think this of the following claim about our cartoon figure: "The figure as a rabbit existed before the tone sounded, but as a duck did not."[13]

This then is our response to the second reaction (described in section I of this chapter) to Kierkegaard's remarks on the God-man paradox. That reaction, it will be recalled, was the one according to which Kierkegaard, whether by intention or by inadvertence, put his finger on a central, devastating self-contradiction in Christian doctrine: that Christ both did and did not exist before the days of Herod.

VI

The cinematic duck-rabbit figure will be helpful in dealing with another matter concerning the notion of the God-man, specifically the dispute between Nestorianism and orthodoxy over whether or not it is proper to say that it was a *man* that the Son of God assumed. Nestorianism holds that it was a man; orthodoxy that it was not. Both Nestorianism and orthodoxy agree that if a man was assumed then there are two persons in the God-man. Nestorianism finds this consequence acceptable; orthodoxy does not.[14]

If one were to ask either a Nestorian or an orthodox theologian to explain why he thinks that the claim that a man was assumed, if true, has the consequence that there are two persons in the

God-man, he would very likely think the explanation only too obvious: of course, the Son of God is a person, and a man is a person. If the Son, who is a person, assumes a man, who is also a person, the result, the God-man, is or consists of two persons, the Son and the man.

But then let us ask what is meant by "assumes" in this explanation? Or better: what must be meant if that which results from the assumption is something consisting of two persons? Clearly, to assume here would mean, roughly, to put on, to don. The explanation, then, tells us that the claim in question has, if true, the consequence of there being two persons in the God-man, because what the claim means, on this explanation, is that one person (the Son) assumed another person (a man), just as, for example, *a man assumes (dons, puts on) his cloak*.

Because both the Nestorian and the orthodox theologian think that the consequence of the claim, if it is true, is that the God-man would consist of two persons, we see two things: (1) that both Nestorian and orthodox construe "assumed" in the claim roughly on the model of "donned,"[15] and (2) that *because* they construe it on this model they both believe the claim, if true, to have the consequence that the God-man consists of two persons.

The claim, if true, *must* have this consequence if "assumed" is construed to mean "donned." But must "assumed" be so construed? Is there a way of construing it, a way of understanding the claim, such that the claim, if true, will not have this consequence? I think that there is. And consideration of the cinematic duck-rabbit can show us what that way is.

Again, what happens on the screen is this: the film opens showing only the figure of a rabbit's head. After five minutes, the head visibly undergoes an alteration such that the rabbit's head, without even for a moment losing the character of a rabbit's head, becomes the figure of a duck-rabbit, or, in other words, *assumes* (is not metamorphosed to) the figure of a duck's head.

Let us now construe "assumed" in the theological claim on the model of "assume" as we have just used it in describing the film.

Construing it in this way, we understand the claim to be that the Son assumed a man, as the figure of the rabbit's head assumed the figure of a duck's head. Now how we must understand this latter case will best be brought out by emphasizing that certain things do *not* occur in the film. (1) A rabbit's head does not appear at the edge of the screen, move toward a duck's at the center of the screen, and come to rest beside or become attached to it, resulting in two figures either juxtaposed or contiguously joined or in two figures formed by two portions of one unbroken line. Should any of these have been the action of the film, and should we then choose to describe the action by saying that the rabbit figure assumed the duck figure, we would be using "assumed" in a sense close to that illustrated by "He assumed his cloak." And that we would be doing so would be shown in this: that two discrete figures would be present not only following, but before and during the assumption. (2) Nor does a rabbit's head appear at the edge of the screen, move toward the duck's head at the center, and either merge with or settle on it and then disappear "in" it—with the result that ("somehow," one is inclined to add) there is a duck-rabbit figure at screen center. Should either of these have been the action, and should we then choose to describe the action by saying that the rabbit figure assumed the duck figure, we would be using "assumed" in a sense still close (but not so close as in case (1)) to that illustrated by "He assumed his cloak." And how close to this sense ours would be is shown in this: (a) that two discrete figures would be present before and during the assumption, and (b) that because, as we would notice while watching the film, one figure would merge with or settle on the other and disappear, with the duck-rabbit figure (somehow) resulting, we would be inclined to say that the rabbit figure would be *in*[16] the duck figure, such that two discrete figures are (queerly) present.

However, in describing the film, as we imagined it to be, by saying that the rabbit figure assumed the duck figure, we are using "assumed" in a sense far removed from that illustrated by "He assumed his cloak." And how far removed it is is shown in this: (a) two discrete figures are present neither before nor during nor following the assumption; (b) there is no inclination to say that, following the assumption, one figure is *in* another, in some *quasi*-intelligible "sense" of "in," such that two discrete figures are (queerly) present. Thus, if we say that the rabbit figure assumed the duck figure, our remark will not be properly understood unless it is taken to involve that assumer and assumed are not, at *any* stage of the action, discrete.

We now see that the cinematic duck-rabbit provides us an alternative model on which to construe "assumed," and so a way of understanding the claim, such that the claim, if true, does not have the consequence that the God-man consists of two persons. Construing "assumed" in this way, we can, I believe, say the following: There is no more reason for thinking that the theological claim, if true, has the consequence that the God-man consists of two persons than there is reason for thinking that the true claim about the film that the rabbit figure assumed a duck figure has the consequence that the duck-rabbit figure consists of two discrete figures.

If this is correct and if our earlier observation is also correct—namely, that because the Nestorian and the orthodox theologian construe "assumed" roughly on the model of "donned," they both believe the claim, if true, to have the consequence that the God-man consists of two persons—then the bone of contention between the two theological camps is removed, and orthodoxy can avoid the difficulties alluded to in note 14 above. For it can say straightway that the Son assumed a man—without fear of falling into the heresy of Nestorianism and so without feeling constrained to look for some alternative way of completing the doctrinal sentence that begins "The Son of God assumed. . . ." "A man," it seems, will do very well.

5 / Free Will and God's Foreknowledge

ON a bright autumn morning two philosophers meet to discuss an issue on which they already have opposing views. With orthodox theology OD holds that the claims that there is an omniscient diety and that there are beings who have free will are logically compatible. NO holds that they are not. Both philosophers agree that the burden lies with NO to make good this denial. Their odd names, by the way, have no significance.

NO: Let's suppose that God knows that you will see the movie *The Apprenticeship of Duddy Kravitz* tonight. If God knows this, then your seeing the movie tonight is unpreventable.

OD: Why "unpreventable"? Why not merely "will not be prevented"?

NO: Well, if in fact you *won't* be prevented from seeing the film, then certainly nothing can be done, nothing can occur, to prevent you. And if this is so, then isn't your seeing the movie unpreventable?

OD: But surely the fact (as we are supposing it to be) that I will not be prevented from seeing the film no more implies that my seeing it is unpreventable than the fact that a windowpane will never be broken implies that it is unbreakable. If God knows that I will see *Duddy Kravitz* tonight, then one possibility under this assumption is that things go in a quite ordinary way. That is, for instance, I see the advertisement for the film in the evening newspaper. Because I am a movie buff and have already read a favorable review or two, I am eager to see this film. Furthermore, tonight I feel like a movie, and nothing presses. So I get into my car and drive to the theater. Nothing out of the way happens. Nothing preventing me or even impeding me occurs or even impends-but-doesn't-occur: no collisions or barely averted collisions, no mugging or just-missed mugging, no explosion or near explosion, no telephone call just before or just after I leave my house to inform me that a near relative has been seriously injured and that I must come to the hospital immediately, no friend arriving for an unexpected visit just moments before or just after my departure, and certainly no mad metaphysical friend who, having got it into his head that he knows that God knows I will see the movie, undertakes by letting the air out of my tires and stealing my distributor cap to show that my seeing the movie is unpreventable. Nothing either known or unknown to me would prevent or even threaten my evening out. Thus if God knows that I will see the film, the object of his knowledge might be just the episode I have described. It is an episode containing nothing that warrants saying that nothing can be done or can occur to prevent my seeing the movie, that justifies saying that my seeing the movie is unpreventable.

NO: But if something were done (though *per hypothesis* will not be done) to prevent you, it would *have* to fail, if God knows that you will see the film. And isn't this tantamount to unpreventability?

OD: If God knows that I will see the film tonight, if the object of his knowledge is the episode described, then only the following can be inferred: that nothing will prevent me from seeing the film. It cannot be inferred that if something were done to prevent me, it would have to fail; for such an attempt, if it were made, might succeed. If, for example, someone were to disable my automobile, I might well be unable to attend the movie. But of course the episode described contains no such attempt.

NO: But look here. If your seeing the movie is not unpreventable, but is instead merely not going to be prevented, then there is a *possibility* (though one that will not be realized) that God will be wrong. But God, we understand, cannot be wrong; there is no possibility that he will be wrong. And so there must be no possibility that you will not see the movie. And if this is so, then how could your seeing the movie be prevented? It must be unpreventable. For if it were merely not going to be prevented, then although God would not be wrong, he could be wrong. In other words, although there would not be falsity, there would be, in Aquinas' phrase, "possibility of falsity in the divine knowledge."

OD: You argue that unless my seeing the movie tonight is unpreventable (instead of merely not going to be prevented) God could be (though would not be) wrong and that since God cannot be wrong, my seeing the movie must be unpreventable. But how could God be wrong? It is true that if an attempt were made to prevent me, it might succeed, or if an accident were to occur, I might be prevented. God knows that no attempt will be made, that no accident will occur. How could God be wrong, then? In his omniscience he knows that none of the perhaps innumerable events that would prevent me will occur. Thus there is no reason here to hold that God can be wrong about my seeing the movie, that there is possibility of falsity in the divine knowledge of that unmomentous event. And yet, let me emphasize, my seeing the film is not unpreventable. If, for instance, someone were to disable my automobile and I learned of this only moments before my intended departure for the cinema, I would no doubt be prevented from seeing the picture. Thus your argument that since God cannot be wrong, my seeing the movie must be unpreventable will not do. We have seen that impossibility of falsity in the divine knowledge consists well with preventability and that what that impossibility requires instead is simple unpreventedness. If an omniscient being knows that a certain stone will never be broken, he may know this infallibly because he knows infallibly that nothing will occur that would break it. It is not necessary that the stone be unbreakable.

NO: I am not convinced that the impossibility of falsity in the divine knowledge does not require unpreventability. I am still inclined to think it does. Now, however, I want to advance another argument, an argument to a rather different conclusion. It is this: that if God knows that you will see the film tonight, you will see it, and since he cannot be wrong, you have no power (are unable) to refrain from seeing the film tonight. For such power is inconceivable—as a power to construct a four-sided triangle is inconceivable. Notice that I am not merely repeating my earlier argument that since God cannot be wrong, your seeing the movie is unpreventable. The word "unpreventable" suggests that no matter what counterforce or obstacle appears, you will attain your goal. My present contention is not that something else is powerless to make you do otherwise. It is that you are powerless to do otherwise. You are powerless because your having the power to do otherwise is just inconceivable. And I have already explained why and in what sense.

OD: Yes; you have. And I grasp your argument. It is that if God knows that I will see the film tonight, then I am unable to do otherwise than see it because the power to do otherwise is in fact the power to bring about a state of affairs that would justify the claim that God erred; and his being wrong is inconceivable. But *is* the power to do otherwise than see the film really what you say it is? Consider again the episode described earlier. If, for instance, a colleague were to telephone just before my departure to invite me to his home a half-hour hence to meet a visiting philosopher whose work interests me, I would no doubt forgo the movie. Clearly, I have the power to do otherwise than see it. Is this power the power to bring about a state of affairs that would justify the claim that God erred? It is, only if its exercise would in fact create such a state of affairs. But what reason is there to think that it would do this? I submit that there is none. There is, rather, the best reason to think that it would not do so—that reason being that God is infallible. Since he is infallible, if I were to exercise my power to do otherwise by going to my colleague's home, so far from my creating a state of affairs justifying the claim that God erred, it would be the case that God knew that I would go to my colleague's home. There seems, then, no reason to deny that I am able to do otherwise than see the movie. For, to repeat, my being able to do otherwise would be the ability to bring about a state of affairs justifying the claim of divine error only if my doing otherwise would bring about such a state of affairs. But there is no reason to think that it would, and the best reason to think that it would not do so.

NO: But now you seem to be suggesting something just absurd. We are agreed for the purposes of this discussion, are we not, that it is a fact that God knows right now on this lovely autumn morning in 1978 that you will see the film *The Apprenticeship of Duddy Kravitz* tonight. But in saying that you can do otherwise, you are suggesting that the fact that God knows this can be nullified. For you say that if you were to exercise your power to do otherwise by, for example, going to your colleague's home for a discussion, it would be the case that God knew that you would go there. You think that you can do something tonight that will make it the case *then* that God will *not* have known something this morning that in fact he *does* know this morning. I am not saying that you think that you can make it the case that God will not know tonight what he knows now—as though you think you can make God utterly forget tonight something he now knows. This too would be absurd, but it is not the thought I am attributing to you. Nor am I contending that you think in effect that you can bring about a state of affairs that would justify the claim that God erred. That was my earlier contention. And it was in fact your response to it that gave rise to my present contention—which, to put it generally, is this. You think that you can make something that was the case earlier not to have been the case then. If it is a fact, as we agree it is, that God knows that you will see the film tonight, it is as absurd to think that you can do otherwise as to think that you can prevent the Second World War fire-bombing of Dresden. For to think that you can do otherwise is to think that you can do something later today that will make it the case that God will not have known this morning what in fact he does know this morning. And that thought, like the one about the fire-bombing of Dresden, is only a specific version of this one: you can make something that was the case earlier not to have been the case then.

OD: As you say, we are agreed for the purposes of this discussion that it is a fact that God knows right now, this morning, that I will see the film this evening. And we see, do we not, that even if that fact could be nullified, my merely being able to do otherwise would not nullify it; that is, to think that I am able to do otherwise is not to suppose that God will not have known this morning what he does know this morning. For that I am able to do otherwise is, of course, consistent with my not doing otherwise—and indeed I will not do otherwise, since God knows that I will see the film. We are agreed about all this.

NO: Indeed, we are. My contention, however, is not that if the fact that God knows could be nullified, your being able to do otherwise would nullify it. My contention is that in thinking that you are able to do otherwise you suppose that the fact that he knows *can* (not will) be nullified. You suppose that you can—not that you will—do something that would make it the case tonight that God will not have known something this morning that in fact he does know this morning.

OD: I'll respond to that. But allow me first a brief review. We agree that God knows this morning that I will see the movie tonight. I am contending that even though God knows this, I can do otherwise. That I can do otherwise is shown, for example, by this: if my colleague were to telephone inviting me to his home for a discussion with an interesting visiting philosopher, I would no doubt change my plans and go to the discussion. Clearly, then, I say, I can do otherwise. Against this you argue that in saying that I can do otherwise tonight I suppose that I can nullify the fact that God knows at this very moment that I will see the film tonight, but that since that fact cannot be nullified, I cannot do otherwise. Now: I *deny* that in saying that I can do otherwise I am supposing that I can nullify that fact. If I were to do otherwise, for instance, go to my colleague's, there would have been this morning no such fact to nullify. In other words, God would not know this morning that I will see the film. So my doing otherwise would not (impossibly) make it the case tonight that he will not have known this morning what he knows this morning. If I were to do otherwise, what he would know this morning is something else, for example, that I will go to my colleague's. And notice that this is consistent with, and so does not abrogate, our initial agreement, namely, that it *is* the case that God knows this morning that I will see the film tonight. For although he would know otherwise if I were to do otherwise, I will not do otherwise.

NO: You seek to show that in saying that you can do otherwise tonight you are not supposing that you can nullify the fact that God knows right now that you will see the movie tonight. To show this you argue that if you *were* to do otherwise tonight, God in his omniscience would know this morning that you would. But is this argument successful? I think not, and I think that I can convince you that it is not by the following analogous case. The city of Dresden was fire-bombed in the Second World War. Since this is so, God of course now knows that it is so. Now if God now knew otherwise, knew, let us say, that Dresden escaped attack altogether, then of course it would be the case that Dresden was not attacked. But since it *is* the case that the city was fire-bombed, it cannot be the case that it escaped fire-bombing. And it is this "cannot" that is important for your position. "Can" and "cannot" in this sense are used by Saint Thomas to present the following reply to an objection in *Summa Theologica:* "God can take away all corruption, mental and physical, from a woman who has lost her [virginity], but he cannot remove the fact that once she did lose it." More generally Thomas would say that God cannot "make what was damaged not to have been damaged." And of course this applies also to Dresden: God can take away all corruption, mental and physical, restoring the city, resurrecting its thousands dead, removing all bitterness, remitting all sins, even, if he chooses, erasing the very memory and record of that dark time, but he cannot remove the fact that the bombing took place, that thousands died, and so on. It cannot, in this sense, be the case that Dresden escaped fire-bombing. And, in the same sense, it cannot be the case that God knows otherwise than that you will see the film tonight. And, as I said, it is this "cannot" that is important for your position. You argue that in saying that you can do otherwise tonight you are not supposing that you can nullify the fact that God knows right now that you will see the film. You argue that if you were to do otherwise God would now know, and have always known, this. But we have seen that it cannot be the case that God now knows this—as we have seen that it cannot be the case now that

Dresden escaped fire-bombing. You must now admit, I think, that you have said nothing allowing you to avoid my earlier charge: that in saying that you can do otherwise you are supposing that you can nullify a fact. I think you will agree, in the light of Saint Thomas's remarks, that not even God can do such a thing. And notice here again that it is vain to retort that if you were to do otherwise God would now know that you would. For, though of course he would know otherwise if you were to do otherwise, the fact is he cannot know otherwise. Just as: of course Dresden would have escaped attack if God now knew that it had, but the fact is it cannot have escaped attack. God's knowing right now, this morning, that you will see the film tonight is—as the Second World War fire-bombing of Dresden is—a *fait accompli*. Notwithstanding contrary-to-*fait-accompli* conditionals.

OD: I accept your claim that it cannot be the case that God knows that I will do otherwise than see the film, as it cannot be the case that Dresden escaped fire-bombing. But you have failed to show that from this claim it follows that I cannot do otherwise. I believe that this cannot be shown and wish now to convince you of this.

To begin let us recall the ordinary episode that is the focus of our discussion. I am a movie buff. I notice an advertisement in the evening newspaper for *The Apprenticeship of Duddy Kravitz*. Having read one or two favorable reviews, I am eager to see the film. Nothing presses and so after dinner I get into my car and drive to the theater. Let us also make the following points explicit about the episode. There is no telephone call inviting me to an evening with a visiting philosopher, no sudden realization that there is a piece of work I ought to do, no fuss over whether the ticket price is too high, no dithering about whether to go to a concert instead, no abatement of my eagerness. In a word, nothing leads me to change my mind or even to reconsider. Now, in this discussion when I say that I can, or am free to, do otherwise than see the film, what I mean is displayed in such considerations as these: if a colleague were to call inviting me to a discussion I would no doubt accept the invitation and go to the discussion; and: if I ceased for some reason (or none) to feel like seeing a movie I would not attend the film. Thus in this discussion I understand that to assert that I am free go do otherwise or that I can do otherwise is to be prepared to declare that at least some of such considerations as those hold true. But if I am prepared to declare this must I, to be consistent, also be prepared to declare the absurdity that I can nullify God's present knowledge that I will see the film? Certainly not. To say, for instance, that if a colleague were to telephone I would go to a discussion is not to suppose that I can nullify God's knowledge. God knows that there will be no telephone call. In his omniscience he knows, to put the point linguistically, that the antecedents of *no* conditionals like the one about the telephone call will be fulfilled. Thus he knows that it will not come to my doing otherwise, to my changing my mind, even to my reconsidering. But, of course, that it will not come to my doing otherwise does not mean that *if* a colleague were to telephone, or *if* my eagerness to see the film abated, I would not do otherwise. God's unannullable knowledge that I will see the film constitutes no reason, then, to deny that I am free to do otherwise. It constitutes a reason to deny only that I will exercise this freedom. God's knowledge that I will see the film is partly characterized by his knowing that nothing will lead me to change my mind—as it is also partly characterized (as we saw in our discussion of unpreventability) by his knowing that nothing will occur to prevent me from seeing the film. Thus his knowledge, though infallible as well as unannullable, is consistent with my freedom or ability to do otherwise, and with the preventability of my seeing the film as well. It is *false* that unless I cannot do otherwise, or lack freedom to do otherwise, God's knowledge must be annullable—as it is false that unless my seeing the movie is unpreventable, his knowledge must be fallible. Of course, I take my point here to apply to any future prima-facie free action, and so I will state it generally. The presumptive truth of countless conditionals of the sort I have instanced, together with God's knowing that their antecedents will remain unfulfilled, is the key to seeing that the freedom and preventability of our future acts are consistent with God's infallible and unannullable foreknowledge of them. That the conditionals are (presumably) true indicates that the future acts in question are free and preventable. That God knows that the antecedents of these conditionals will remain unfulfilled (1) means that he knows that we will not exercise our freedom to act otherwise and also will not be prevented doing what we do, and (2) thus guarantees that the freedom and preventability of our actions are consistent with the infallibility and unannullability of his prior knowledge of those actions. And if I may be permitted a brief diagnostic remark: What appears to make us fail to grasp the foregoing point is our myopic unmindfulness that the one item of God's knowledge continuously before us in this discussion—his knowledge that I will see the film tonight—lies in his knowledge of an episode, and, indeed, of the great episode that is the time of the world. We thus fail to see the relevance of his knowing that nothing will lead me to exercise my freedom and that nothing will occur to prevent me.

NO: It seems to me that the point you make concerning the presumptive truth of those countless conditionals and God's knowing that their antecedents will not be fulfilled has merit, but less merit than you suppose. You succeed in revealing the inadequacy of my argument from unannullability. But I believe that in revealing it you inadvertently suggest the vulnerability of your own position. First, let me describe the merit I see in your point, and then I will advance an argument to wound your compatibilism direly.

The merit of your point is revealed in our movie case. You have shown that in saying that you can act otherwise you are not supposing that you can nullify God's present knowledge that you will see the film tonight. You have shown this by pointing out that although if one or another of certain contingencies occurred you *would* do otherwise, the thought that you would does not involve the supposition that you can annul God's present knowledge, because his knowledge consists partly in knowing infallibly that no such contingency will occur. Thus, though freedom is present, infallible knowledge that it will not be exercised preserves unannullability.

Your point makes it clear that the incompatibilist position, which I still espouse, cannot be proved by arguing simply from the unannullability of God's infallible foreknowledge of some putatively free act when the act is considered in isolation from its history and circumstances—and particularly in isolation from what we might call the negative aspects of its history and circumstances. You have shown how the ignored history and circumstances can be marshaled to rout such simple arguments. Moreover, your point has some significance outside the present discussion. A. N. Prior accepts an argument (which he takes from Saint Thomas) that is essentially the same as mine, an argument from the present unpreventability of God's foreknowledge. You will find his treatment of it in his "The Formalities of Omniscience."[1] Because Prior is as oblivious as I have been of the relevance of history and circumstances, I believe your point to be as devastating to his (and Thomas's) argument as to mine. Yet, however worthwhile this result may be, I also believe that you overestimate the merit of your point.

You have reminded us of the importance to our discussion of God's knowledge of (as you put it) the great episode that is the time of the world. That great episode presumably includes every event and situation, past, present, and future, from the most momentous to the least significant: wars, periods of peace, weddings, beddings, huffs, reconciliations, the small business of common life, an unminded turn of head, a trillion trillion footfalls, the precise lie or motion at each moment of every blade of grass and grain of sand, the fall of every raindrop, its shape, its change of shape. And God's knowledge of all this is "before all worlds" and "from everlasting to everlasting." From before the world was made God knew there would be saxophones! As I try to make vivid the infinitesimal detail and infinite scope of what he knows and has known eternally, the feeling grows that what I am trying to make vivid is just unintelligible!

OD: What you are coming to see is that his omniscience is a mystery. This has always been recognized and admitted by godly men.

NO: Don't mistake me. I do not mean that we cannot comprehend, or, so to speak, surround with our minds or imaginations, the limitlessness of what he knows. This seems to be the awed thought of the psalmist when he says "God, how hard it is to grasp your thoughts! How impossible to count them! I could no more count them than I could the sand" (Ps. 139:17–18, *Jerusalem Bible*). Nor do I mean that though we understand quite well *that* he knows what he knows, we can not understand *how* he knows it. This seems to be the psalmist's thought in an earlier verse of the same psalm, the verse "Such knowledge is beyond my understanding, a height to which my mind cannot attain." (A later verse contains the suggestion that the psalmist *does* understand how God knows. I will take this up in a moment.) What I do mean is that we do not understand the notion of omniscience, because no model, no analogy, will yield a satisfactory sense for it.[2]

OD: Why do you say "a satisfactory sense"? Are there, then, some *un*satisfactory senses that some analogies or models yield?

NO: Yes; there are—unsatisfactory for your compatibilism, that is. If God's knowing from before all worlds the "great episode" in its smallest detail is modeled, for example, on a dishonest gambler's knowing beforehand how a prize-fight will turn out, then of course "God's foreknowledge" is in that case intelligible, but its intelligibility is clearly unsatisfactory, because then we must understand the great episode to be fixed, determined in advance, foreordained, in its every detail. Some of the psalmist's words in 139:16 suggest this understanding of God's foreknowledge. Addressing his Lord the psalmist says (according to the *Jerusalem Bible's* translation): "You had scrutinized my every action, all were recorded in your book, my days listed and determined [or "formed" in some translations and glossed as "fixed" in one Catholic commentary], even before the first of them occurred." The clause "my days listed and determined [formed, fixed]" suggests that the psalmist would be prepared to model "God's foreknowledge" on the gambler's—the understanding of both formed by the realization or supposition of a pre-arranging, or in gamblers' parlance, a fix.

Another model yielding a sense for "God's omniscience" (or "foreknowledge") that is unsatisfactory for your position is the astronomer's knowing beforehand the times of the sunrise and sunset and of coming eclipses. If this case provides the model, the understanding of "God's foreknowing" the great episode involves supposing the operation of universal causation, as understanding the astronmer's knowing involves realizing that certain causal factors are operating. It is noteworthy that Saint Thomas accepted this understanding of "God's foreknowledge" of the great episode and concluded that neither God nor any being could have literal *fore*knowledge of it since much of the great episode is not under the sway of causal factors, as the motions of the heavenly bodies are under their sway. Moreover, Thomas made explicit how "God's foreknowledge" so understood would be unsatisfactory (to himself and to you).

Such foreknowledge (requiring as it does that "all take place necessarily") "would destroy free choice and there would be no need to ask advice" (*Truth*, Q II, art. 12). The astronomer model fares no better for your position than does the gambler model.

OD: I agree that neither of these models yields a sense I can accept. But I am not constrained to suppose either of them. There are others. Consider again verse sixteen of Psalm 139. The first clause is this: "You had scrutinized my every action." The context makes it clear that this scrutiny "had" taken place prior to the time of the psalmist's actions. Now one may well say, "How can actions that are not taking place be scrutinized? If the maestro is scrutinizing (not just 'thinking about') his pupil's fingering, surely the pupil must *be* fingering!" It might seem, then, that scrutinizing requires that there be no temporal separation between it and its object. But is this so? Can't an action be scrutinized in thought—as it can be contemplated in thought? If one contemplates one's next move, that move need not, indeed, cannot then be occurring. And may not a baseball batting-coach scrutinize in thought or in his mind's eye his slumping slugger's swing? And if so, the player of course need not then be swinging. In any case, the philosopher Nelson Pike provides us a model that yields acceptable senses for both "God's scrutiny" and "God's foreknowledge." The model is that of a crystal-ball gazer. "God's scrutiny" from before all worlds of the great episode is intelligible on the model of the gazer's fore-seeing events by gazing at the ball. And "God's foreknowledge" of the great episode is intelligible, as "the gazer's foreknowledge" of events is intelligible—the understanding of both being formed by the supposition of a pre-scrutiny, a fore-seeing, of what is foreknown. Of course one need not think that such pre-viewing is possible in the case of the gazer. No doubt one is best advised to treat crystal-ball gazing as purest flummery. But even a humbug can have (mere) intelligibility and so be a model for the intelligibility of something that is not a humbug. Moreover, this model avoids the freedom-destroying suppositions of the gambler and astronomer models: the gazer is not supposed either to mysteriously foreordain or fix events or by gazing into the ball to apprise himself of "the determining causes" of events.

NO: I agree with you about that. The model of the gazer certainly avoids those suppositions. Nevertheless, I think that the case does not yield a satisfactory sense for "God's foreknowledge"—not because it involves some freedom-destroying supposition or other, but because, if it exhibits knowledge at all, it does not exhibit knowledge of the required kind. I will explain.

Suppose the gazer has never been wrong in any of his thousands of predictions. Customers flock to him. "Do you wish to know whether your son will return safely from a summer visit to Europe? Consult the swami; he can tell you. He never fails." People say the swami *knows*. They don't say this at first, of course, but only after some few, or many, successful predictions. Have they merely fallen into a way of talking, a way of regarding the predictions, or does the swami really know? If he really knows, then his very first prediction, as well as the others, was surely knowledge—followed somewhat later by the general admission that this is so. And if the first prediction was knowledge, then it was so independently of the subsequent successes. It would be knowledge even if no subsequent prediction were fulfilled.

OD: I suppose that you are right. If saying that the swami knows is not just a way of talking that people fall into because of his continuous success, then his first prediction is knowledge independently of later success. And so it is knowledge even if no one ever sees that it is. But that is not an impossibility. In fact such things are no doubt commonplace. Surely we must believe that a great many things occur that go unrecognized. After all, full many a flower is born to blush unseen.

NO: Ah, yes. But what is the flower in question? What does that first prediction's being knowledge amount to? It amounts only to (1) a pronouncement and (2) the coming to pass of what is pronounced. A *basis* for the pronouncement is not involved, nor, surely, is certainty. It would be difficult to imagine the swami confident on his first try.

OD: It would be difficult. But why do you say there is no basis for the pronouncement? Of course there is. The vision induced by gazing at the crystal ball is the basis. Were you thinking that the swami's first pronouncement, that the knowledge expressed in it, amounted to mere correct guessing? You said that there is the pronouncement and the coming to pass of what is pronounced—like, "The coin will come up heads," and it comes up heads. But guessing doesn't necessarily or even normally involve visions. And, more importantly, it doesn't involve that the guesser has a special power. The swami, however, if he isn't a fake, has a special power. He is a receiver and transmitter. On being consulted he puts himself in a state favorable to foretelling the future. By gazing at the ball he induces visions. This he has the power to do. And his power is the more remarkable for the fact that his visions bear on the questions and concerns of his client—and still more remarkable for the fact (as we are supposing it to be) that his visions never lead him astray. On their basis he is always right. Now, this is a far cry from mere guessing, and a far cry from merely guessing right.

NO: Indeed it is. I am grateful for the clarification. But however far a cry it is from correct guessing, I still wish to maintain that it is not knowledge, or not, at any rate, knowledge of the right sort. You say the swami has a special power, and you characterize him as a receiver and transmitter. All right. He can induce "messages" in himself in the form of visions and announce their content. But now let us externalize the internal in the way Wittgenstein liked to. You remember that he said, "We could perfectly well, for our purposes, replace every process of imagining by a process of looking at an object or by painting, drawing or modelling; and every process of speaking to oneself by speaking aloud or by writing." I think that we, too, for *our* purposes can do this. First, then, instead of imagining the swami to have visions and to announce their content, suppose he is simply *moved to say something*. He gazes at the ball and *finds himself saying* (as before he found himself envisioning) what serves correctly to answer his client's questions and concerns. Suppose also that sometimes he does this while alone. Sometimes he pronounces over his crystal ball in solitude and then steps into the adjoining room, where his client waits, and repeats for him what he pronounced. The swami's repetitions to his clients are based on what he has pronounced in solitude. But he can as well pronounce in the client's presence and when he does this what he says, unlike his repetitions, is based on nothing.

OD: If the pronouncements are always correct one may well think that they are reflections, or preflections, of the events they are about. I mean that the events to come may in some strange way be a causal basis of the pronouncements.

NO: Well, as Prior (following Jonathan Edwards) responded to a similar proposal, "this means more than ever that [an event's] future coming to pass is beyond prevention, since it has already *had consequences* which its opposite could not have." And of course you are eager to avoid unpreventability.

OD: Yes, yes. Then I withdraw the suggestion. I will go along with your claim that the swami's pronouncement has no basis or ground. It does not follow from this, however, that his pronouncement does not evince his knowledge. As Nelson Pike says, "there are relatively clear cases in which the verb 'knows' applies even though the knower does not have evidence or grounds for his belief." And I agree with Pike that one such case is that of the crystal-ball gazer.

NO: I will not deny that the swami is a knower. But it is important to be clear about *how* he is a knower, about how the verb "know" applies in his case. It is important to see that regardless of how he discovered or acquired his powers of pronouncing, his attitude to his early pronouncements will naturally be decidedly skeptical. Indeed, if we imagine that one day he simply finds himself pronouncing, his first reaction would surely be one of befuddlement—a befuddlement that, as time goes on and more and more pronouncements come true, becomes a skepticism-turning-to-confidence. From the beginning his pronouncements are a source of information, correct information, about the future. But he doesn't know the future. He is a mere vessel, a container. He can no more be said to evince a knowledge of the future in his pronouncements than can a fruit jar because slips of paper bearing correct information about the future mysteriously appear in it from time to time. As he comes to trust the pronouncements, however, he can be said to know. Given thousands of pronouncements all borne out by events, this would be the natural language to adopt by anyone who appreciated the facts. But it is crucial to see that the swami does not know at the beginning; he is just a vessel of correct information then. Nor of course do he and others gradually learn that he knew at the beginning. They only come to see that his mysterious pronouncements were the source of information. And only in coming to trust the pronouncements can they—the swami included—be said to know. As a vessel the swami is not (ever) a knower: his pronouncements do not evince, express, or demonstrate knowledge. As a keeper of the vessel, as a hearer of those pronouncements, he comes to know, just as his clients come to know: by coming to trust the pronouncements, they all fall into applying the verb "know" to themselves.

This is the logical situation that makes it folly to use the case of the crystal-ball gazer as a model for the understanding or sense of "God's foreknowledge." To do so would require one to think that though God contains everlasting prefigurations—whether one thinks of these as pronouncements or as visions doesn't matter—of the great episode to come, he cannot be said to know that the prefigurations are correct until at least some of that episode has passed. That is, though he is from everlasting a vessel of correct information about the future, only latterly does he come to know the future. This consideration is by itself fatal to the gazer cases's candidacy for modelhood. There is, however, an additional reason to reject the case, and this reason too is fatal by itself.

Modeled on the gazer case, God's foreknowledge must be based on an ever-growing body of prefigurations-borne-out and so be merely a flowering of God's trust in prefigurations still unconfirmed. Thus there would be introduced "the possibility of falsity" in the divine foreknowledge and therefore something that comes too close for comfort to downright credulity. The thought of God placing his trust in everlasting prefigurations because some of them have been borne out by events makes him decidedly less than infallible and too much a trusting soul. Such an ingredient is inconceivable in the character of a perfect deity.

We have, then, two excellent reasons to reject the case of the gazer, either of which is fatal to its candicacy. First, the gazer has no knowledge until at least some of the events he envisions or "pronounces" have come to pass. Second, he and his clients—however natural and apt the application of "know" to their case may be—betray something too close to credulity.

Earlier I said that I was going to produce an argument that would grievously wound your compatibilism. The foregoing examination of three prominent candidates for modelhood is a preparation for this argument, which is brief. It is that the sense or understanding of "God's foreknowledge" yielded by the various models that have emerged in the history of this problem, perhaps even from the time of the psalmist, are unsatisfactory because they involve either freedom-destroying suppositions or knowledge of the wrong kind. This argument is not fatal to your position because it does not rule out the possibility of producing a quite satisfactory model. But it does seriously damage your position because it forces you to make two important concessions. First, you must concede that it is quite possible that the claim that from everlasting God foreknew the great episode in its every detail does not make sense in a way that would, if the claim were true, attribute the requisite kind of knowledge to God and also leave our freedom unimpaired. Second, you must concede that unless such a model is found there is *no* reason to think that this claim does make sense in the requisite way.

OD: I appreciate the need for a viable model, but I am not now able to produce one. There is, however, a very influential one that we have not mentioned. It is the model that both Boethius and Saint Thomas adopted: the model of seeing what is presently happening. I have not mentioned it because it makes God's knowledge of the future into something that is not literally *fore* knowledge (as Thomas himself acknowledges in *Truth*) and my position has all this while concerned foreknowledge literally understood. Perhaps, however, to save my compatibilism I must resort to it.

NO: Have you read Anthony Kenny's and Prior's trenchant criticisms of this model?[3] It seems to me that what they say delivers a near knock-out punch to the Thomist model. Instead of reciting their criticisms, however, I will add a blow of my own.

Thomas says that "the relation of the divine knowledge to anything whatsoever is like that of present to present." He explains this by an example: "If someone were to see many people walking successively down a road during a given period of time, in each part of that time he would see as present some of those who walk past, so that in the whole period of his watching he would see as present all of those who walked past him. Yet he would not simultaneously see them all as present, because the time of his seeing is not completely simultaneous. However, if all his seeing could exist at once, he would simultaneously see all the passers-by as present, even though they themselves would not all pass as simultaneously present" (*Truth*, Qu. 2, art. 12). Now what is puzzling in this passage are these two clauses: "because the time of his seeing is not completely simultaneous" and "if all his seeing could exist at once." What would it be for all his seeing to exist at once, to be completely simultaneous? I will suggest two plausible ways of understanding this, rejecting the first way and accepting the second. The first is this. If we think of the watcher's seeing taking place "at once," we might think of him opening his eyes only for an instant, a reverse blink, or (what comes to the same) we might think of the scene suddenly and very briefly illuminated by lightning on a black night. In either case the movement would be "frozen" as in a still photograph of action in an athletic contest. This will not do as a way of understanding Thomas, however, for what is seen in just an instant is only an instant of the action. Moreover, when Thomas speaks of the watcher's seeing, he is speaking of a seeing that continues for, say, a quarter of an hour. The watcher on his park bench watches for fifteen minutes as people stroll by. Now Thomas's idea is that we think of that quarter-hour's seeing as telescoped into simultaneity. What one would see, then, is not an instant of an action, but all of the action—not a tossed blackboard eraser caught in mid-flight across a room, but its whole flight from beginning to end.

But what is it to see the flight of the eraser, a flight taking, let's say, one-and-a-half seconds, in less time than the flight itself takes? What is it to see that brief action "at once" so that the time of seeing is "completely simultaneous"? In order for the time of seeing to be completely simultaneous, the flight itself, all one-and-a-half seconds of it, would have to be, in

Thomas's phrase, "as present." The flight itself would have to be as though at once. It would have to be as though the eraser were in my hand, about to leave my hand, ever so close to my hand—and to make a long story short, everywhere in its flight simultaneously. And I can think of no better way to understand this than to think, not of a sports-page "action still," but of a time exposure. In a time exposure the whole flight of the eraser would be "as present"—the eraser would be pictured as everywhere on its flight at once.

But if to one whose time of seeing the eraser flying is completely simultaneous the eraser's flight is as like a time-exposure photograph, then he does not see the eraser flying. He does not see it moving. He does not, to generalize, see anything in motion: clouds drifting, geese flying, people walking by. He has only a time exposure of it all.

Thus the model Thomas provides makes unacceptable sense of "God's foreknowledge." If we take it seriously, it requires us to think that in "the vision of divine knowledge" nothing is moving, as nothing is moving in a time-exposure photograph. And of course this is a result that Thomas would not want, for it constitutes a drastic improverishment of God's knowledge. His model succeeds, then, no better than the others we have examined.

OD: I gladly abjure it with the others. But at present I have none to put in its place. In any case, you have convinced me of this much: that when another candidate does come to mind, it must be rigorously and patiently tested and, unless it survives testing, I still lack warrant to say that "God's foreknowledge" of the great episode makes acceptable sense.

Here the dialogue ends. Let us suppose that OD and NO fail to find a satisfactory model because there is none. Let us suppose that "God's foreknowledge" of the great episode in all its turnings, in its every detail, has no acceptable sense. If this is true, then an important doctrine of classical theology cannot be true. It does not follow, however, that what can be discerned in Scripture concerning God's foreknowledge cannot be true, for classical theological doctrine may not accurately represent scriptural content, even though its intention may be to do so. And indeed there does seem to have been a slip here between the scriptural cup and the theological lip. It seems, for instance, that when the Lord bade Jeremiah to stand in the court of the Temple and to repeat the Lord's threat that unless the people of the towns of Judah turn from evil ways, he will bring disaster on them, the Lord *did not know* whether they would do so, for he says, "Perhaps they will listen and each turn from his evil way" (Jer. 26:3; cf. 36:3). Again, when the Lord stays Abraham's hand against Isaac it seems that only then, *and not before*, does he know Abraham truly fears God, for the Lord says, "Do not harm [Isaac], for now I know you fear God" (Gen. 22:12; cf. Deut. 13:3). Nor will it do to protest that the Lord really means that now *Abraham* knows—as though the Lord knew all along that Abraham would remain firm in his faithfulness and the whole point of the command to sacrifice Isaac was to apprise Abraham of his own spiritual condition. Surely the episode is (as Scripture describes it) a "test" of Abraham to allow the Lord to determine the depth or reality of his faith and the ". . . now I know . . ." a straightforward announcement of that determination. A third case in point is this. The Lord tells Jeremiah that in dealing with the nations he sometimes changes his mind and does the opposite of what he had intended to do. If a nation on which he intends to confer good does something that displeases him he changes his mind and withholds the good. And, conversely, if a wicked nation which he intends to destroy abandons its evil ways he changes his mind and withholds punishment (Jer. 18:1–11). What are we to make of the Lord's intention to destroy a wicked nation if we suppose that he knew quite certainly even while he intended it that he would not do it? "To intend to do X while knowing full well one will not do X," if it describes a possibility of mind at all, surely does not describe one attributable to the Lord. Rather, the text shows the justice of the Lord's comparison of himself with a potter who "whenever the vessel he was making came out wrong, as happens with the clay handled by potters, he would start afresh and work it into another vessel, as potters do" (Jer. 18:4). The potter does not know in advance, but only comes to see as he works on it, that a particular vessel must be destroyed. No more does the Lord know in advance, but only comes to see as he deals with his creatures, who are sometimes rebellious and follow their own whims, that in this instance or that he must withhold a blessing that he had earlier intended to bestow.

Against the thrust of these Scriptures and of the dialogue between OD and NO, classical theology has an uphill fight on its hands to show that the doctrine of God's omniscience as it conceives it is both intelligible and scripturally justified. But if it does not succeed, as I think it cannot, there is no great matter for the Jew or Christian, because even if classical theology fails in this task, the believer has no reason to think that from eternity God could not know that his plan for his creation would be fulfilled. That plan (they must believe) he will *bring* to pass. For instance, Christians can believe that the time of Christ's second coming is known to the Father because they understand that the Father will send him and knows when he will send him. But they have no reason to think that the divine plan includes minutiae like the fall of a raindrop, an unminded turn of head, or even a particular episode of rebelliousness and therefore no reason to think that God must foreknow such things from eternity or even to think that eternal "foreknowledge" of such things is intelligible.

6 / The General Resurrection

I

WE have it from John Locke that "he that shall, with a little attention, reflect on the resurrection, and consider that divine justice shall bring to judgement, at the last day, the very same persons, to be happy or miserable in the other, who did well or ill in this life, will find it, perhaps, not easy to resolve with himself what makes the same man, or wherein identity consists."

In this chapter I will, with a little attention, reflect on the resurrection. I will do this, however, not in order to resolve with myself what makes the same man, or wherein identity consists. Instead, I hope to determine whether certain arguments that do purport to resolve this question, or that presuppose it already resolved, succeed in making trouble for the doctrine of resurrection—or, rather, for a certain version of this doctrine.

The version I have in mind is set out in the following passage from a book on Christian dogma, *The Christian Hope*, by T. A. Kantonen. Kantonen is here summarizing the views of two Protestant theologians, Paul Althaus and Karl Heim. "'The Christian faith knows nothing about an immortality of the person. That would mean a denial of death. . . . There is existence after death only by way of... resurrection.' There is no immortality of the soul but a resurrection of the whole person, body and soul, from death." Again, "when we die... we pass into nothingness. There is nothing in man that is capable of resisting the destructive power of death.... The Bible does not distinguish between man and the beasts on the ground that man has an immortal soul while the beasts do not. Men, beasts, even plants, are alike in death." "It is only when we are annihilated that we can be truly resurrected."[1]

This, then, is the version of the doctrine of resurrection that will occupy us. The sort of trouble supposedly raised for it by the arguments we will examine is indicated by Antony Flew in the following rhetorical question. Regarding the doctrine as teaching the "reconstitution of the person" Flew says, "might not a sceptic argue that reconstituted Flew was only an imitation of the Flew that had been destroyed; and hence that I would not be justified in looking forward to the things that would happen to him as things that would happen to me?" For, as Flew remarks in another place, "words like 'you,' 'I,' 'person,' 'somebody,' 'Flew,' 'woman,'—though very different in their several particular functions—are all used to refer in one way or another to objects (the pejorative flavour of this word should here be discounted) which you can point at, touch, hear, see and talk to. Person words refer to people. And how can such objects as people survive physical dissolution?"

How, indeed? And if they cannot, then would not Flew's skeptic be quite right to argue that reconstituted Flew would be only an imitation of the Flew that is destroyed?

The view presented in the Kantonen passage quoted above, however, is the view of men who regard people as existing, as it were, in two installments. This is a view which, given their interpretation of Scripture, they regard as based on God's word. They regard themselves as having been given to understand by an unimpeachable authority something about human beings (something, moreover, that can be learned *only* from that authority): namely, that human beings are one-gap-inclusive creatures, that their identity survives a gap in time.

For those holding the Althaus-Heim view, then, Flew's skeptic is operating on the mistaken presupposition that persons are not gap inclusive. In thinking that a person cannot survive death and dissolution, the skeptic is, by their lights, making a mistake analogous to that of thinking that the first installment (in the current issue of a periodical) of a two-installment story is and cannot but be the whole story. And in thinking that the "reconstituted" Flew is a mere imitation or likeness of Flew—and so, of course, numerically distinguishable from Flew—the skeptic is, in the Althaus-Heim view, making a mistake analogous to that of thinking that the second installment (to appear in a future issue) is and cannot but be a second story.

But of course the notion that people are one-gap inclusive is wildly counterintuitive. I have seen a young philosopher react to the notion by thumping himself on the chest and saying with intensity, "Stories in two installments certainly! But not this! Not flesh and blood!" One would like more, however, than an intuitive reaction. One wants to ask what gives rise to it. Is what gives rise to it something that constitutes or will yield conclusive reasons to support the reaction? If so, then the skeptic can *conclude*, and not merely claim, that alleged resurrectees could be no more than simulacra, for he will be able to show that the intuition that people are not gap inclusive is a true one.

II

What argument can we find to justify this intuition? Perhaps Flew's argument in his "Locke and the Problem of Personal Identity"[2] will do. There Flew appeals to the Lockean principle that "one thing cannot have two beginnings of existence, nor two things one beginning. . . . That, therefore, that had one beginning, is the same thing; and that which had a different beginning in time and place from that, is not the same, but diverse." From this principle it is concluded that any person produced on the day of resurrection, however indistinguishable he may be from one who has died, cannot be that person who died. Flew's thinking is that any person produced on the day of resurrection will have "a different beginning in time" from that of any person who died, and since "one thing cannot have two beginnings of existence," no person produced on the day of resurrection can be (one and the same person as) some person born at an earlier time.

This reasoning sustains Flew's conclusion, however, only if it is supposed that the production of any person on the day of resurrection and someone's birth much earlier must be counted two beginnings. It is clear that they must be if persons are not gap inclusive. But if they are one-gap inclusive, then the production of the person on the day of resurrection cannot be counted a different beginning—not at least in a sense that implies the production of a second person. For if people are one-gap inclusive, then their birth is their only "beginning of existence" and their later "production" on the day of resurrection is a resumption of existence or life—as the start, after an intermission, of the performance of the second act of a two-act play is a resumption of the play or of the performance of the play, not a "different beginning," the beginning of a second performance or of a second play.

Flew's use of Locke's one-beginning principle is thus seen to fail. By applying it he seeks to show that no alleged resurrectee could be someone already born and deceased. But the principle cannot be used to show this and will seem to lend itself to such use only if what is to be proved is assumed, namely, that people are not gap inclusive or—what is here tantamount to this—cannot have a resurrection life. If it is assumed that they are not gap inclusive, then of course an alleged resurrectee would have "a different beginning" and thus could not be some one already born and deceased. But since this assumption of non-gap inclusiveness finds no support in Flew's argument, his argument comes to naught. It cannot be used to justify the intuition that people are not one-gap inclusive.

A second argument that might accomplish this end was suggested to me by Peter van Inwagen. It is this: When a person suffers death and dissolution he ceases to exist—as a piece of chalk worn completely away by writing ceases to exist. What has ceased to exist cannot exist again. Thus when a piece of chalk ceases to exist no piece of chalk that afterward comes to exist can be that earlier piece. Its existence can include no gap. And if one is disinclined to accept this, it is most likely because one is construing "ceases to exist" on some palliative model, like "goes over to the 'other side.'"

The principle involved here is that for any entity you please, when it ceases to exist it cannot exist again. Therefore, for any entity you please, its existence can include no gap. I will begin by accepting this principle.

When a shoe, a ship, a cabbage, a king ceases to exist there is for it no existing again. The principle holds too for temporal entities such as the performance of a play. Let us suppose that last night there was a performance of Dylan Thomas's *Under Milk Wood* at the Fine Arts Center and that the performance began at eight o'clock and ended at 10:30. The temporal entity that is that performance began to exist at eight o'clock and continued to exist until 10:30, when it ceased to exist. And had it ceased to exist at some time during that two-and-a-half-hour period, it could not of course have come to exist again. Our principle ensures this.

But what then of the fifteen-minute intermission that (let us suppose) interrupted the performance from 8:55 until 9:10? Did not the performance cease to exist at 8:55 and begin to exist again at 9:10? If our principle is unexceptionable, as we have supposed, then the answer must be no. That temporal entity, the performance, began to exist at eight o'clock and continued in existence until 10:30, and only then ceased to exist. Our principle requires us to say that the performance did not cease to exist at the intermission, for if it had, it could not have continued after the intermission. We have to say, then, that the intermission interrupted the performance, but not the performance's existence. This may seem a strange remark, and yet it must be allowed if the principle is not to be confuted by such cases as intermission-inclusive performances. How are we to understand the distinction between the performance and the performance's existence, such that the intermission interrupts the one but leaves the other unaffected? Well, we do make such a distinction. If someone rushes into the lobby of the Fine Arts Center at 8:55 and, finding a group of people there, asks if the performance is going on, one may wonder what he is asking. Two possibilities are likely. He may want to know whether the performance has begun; or he may want to know whether the performance is then in intermission. If the former, then the answer is "Yes, the performance is going on," even though at 8:55 it is in intermission. If the latter, then the answer is "No, the performance is not going on," since it is in intermission. Our distinction between the performance and the performance's existence, such that the intermission interrupts the performance and leaves its existence unaffected, echoes the fact that one can truly say, even during intermission, that the performance is going on (the performance's existence is unaffected by the intermission), and one can truly say, during intermission, that the performance is not going on (the performance is interrupted by the intermission). Thus the fact of the intermission provides no counterexample to confute the principle: even such entities as intermission-inclusive performances do not confute, but instead express the principle that for any entity you please, when it ceases to exist it cannot exist again. For an intermission is not a ceasing of the performance's existence.

What now of the case of a person? If the principle is, as we are supposing, unobjectionable, then his case too expresses it, does not confute it.

"Well, then," says an adversary, "your game is up, isn't it. You allow that the case of a person, too, expresses the principle. This is as much as to admit that the existence of a person, like that of a piece of chalk or that of an intermission-inclusive performance, can include no gap. Thus the intuition that people are not gap inclusive is justified."

On the contrary the intuition is not justified by the admission that the existence of a person can include no gap. For this admission is consistent with the theologian's contention that people are one-gap inclusive—just as admitting that the existence of last night's performance of *Under Milk Wood* can include no gap is consistent with the performance's including an intermission.

The principle under examination does not, any more than does Locke's one-beginning principle, justify the intuition. Gap inclusiveness is consistent with continuance in existence, just as it is consistent with having one beginning.

Here an adversary again intervenes. "You claim that the admission that the existence of a person can include no gap does not justify the intuition that people are not gap inclusive, because (you say) that admission is consistent with the theologian's contention that people are one-gap inclusive—as the admission that the existence of the performance can include no gap is consistent with the performance's including an intermission. But surely a brief second look at the matter shows that this is incorrect. It can easily be shown that the claim that a person's existence can include no gap is *not* consistent with the theologian's contention that people are one-gap inclusive. To say that a person's existence can include no gap is of course an application of our principle that whatever ceases to exist cannot exist again. Now let us apply this principle carefully to the case of a person, as was done in the argument suggested by van Inwagen: 'When a person suffers death and dissolution he ceases to exist. What has ceased to exist cannot exist again.' If the principle is accepted and given its natural and proper application to the case of a person—the application just given it—then of course a person's death and dissolution *are* his ceasing to exist, and since whatever ceases to exist cannot exist again, his ceasing to exist is his *end*. And so no one who comes to exist later can be that person. Thus acceptance of the principle, together with its proper application to the case of a person, *does* justify our intuition that people are not gap inclusive."

Our response to this can be put disjunctively: (1) If in suffering death and dissolution a person ceases to exist, then it is not indubitable that in ceasing to exist he cannot exist again; or (2) if whatever ceases to exist cannot exist again, then it is not indubitable that in suffering death and dissolution a person ceases to exist. Both disjunct (1) and disjunct (2) question the applicability of the principle to the case of a person, but each in a different way and for a different reason. Disjunct (1) grants that in death and dissolution a person ceases to exist but doubts that it follows from this that he cannot exist again. Thus (1) says that perhaps the principle is not universally true, that perhaps a person's death and dissolution constitute an exception to it. Disjunct (2) grants that the principle is universally true but doubts that a person's death and dissolution constitute a ceasing to exist. Thus (2) says that perhaps the principle is universally true but that perhaps a person's death and dissolution are (not an exception to it, but) simply an irrelevant phenomenon.

To summarize, the argument under examination is this: a person's death and dissolution entails that he ceases to exist; his ceasing to exist entails that he cannot exist again. Our disjunctive response to this argument questions either its first or its second entailment. Disjunct (1) places a question mark after the second entailment; disjunct (2) places one after the first.

But of course thus far we have not offered reasons for affirming either of these disjuncts; we have offered no reasons to doubt either of these entailments. To reasons we now must turn.

Turning first to the second entailment, what reasons are there to doubt that it holds if the first entailment is taken to hold? That is, what reasons are there to doubt that a person's ceasing to exist entails that he cannot exist again if one allows that a person's death and dissolution entails that he ceases to exist? To state the reasons requires us first to notice that there is a solid linguistic reason for thinking that the first entailment does hold. For "a person's death and dissolution entails that he ceases to exist" seems simply a way of saying that talk of death and dissolution and talk of ceasing to exist, or of ceasing to be, are roughly equivalent. Certainly the entailment's ring of truth is due to this rough equivalence. Such lines as these speak, of course, of death: "few could know when Lucy ceased to be"; "when I have fears that I may cease to be"; "to be or not to be."

But if the first entailment reports this rough linguistic equivalence of "death and dissolution" and "ceasing to exist," what is the status of the second entailment—that a person's ceasing to exist entails that he cannot exist again? It may seem to report a connection such that lines like those quoted above imply that resumption of existence, rising to life again, is impossible. However, those lines—as well as their cease-to-be phrases—seem to be neutral on the point. An examination of their contexts confirms this. The contexts reveal a variety of beliefs and attitudes concerning ceasing to exist—a variety that attests to the adaptability and hence the neutrality of cease-to-exist phrases or, in other words, of the notion of a person's ceasing to exist. The context of "when I have fears that I may cease to be," a sonnet of Keats, suggests that the author felt that his ceasing to be would be irrevocable, final ("I shall never look upon thee more"). On the other hand, the context of "and few could know when Lucy ceased to be," the Wordsworth Lucy poem, contains the suggestion of bereavement and loss, but not necessarily of irrevocable loss ("but she is in her grave and, oh, the difference to me"). Concerning the possibility of resurrection or a resumption of existence the poem seems as neutral as cease-to-be phrases themselves do. The context of "to be or not to be," Hamlet's famous soliloquy, carries a different suggestion still, for it expresses Hamlet's suspicion that even after ceasing to be, one might continue in existence and continue to suffer ("the dread of something after death," ills "we know not of").

That the notion of a person's ceasing to exist accommodates this range of beliefs and attitudes strongly suggests its neutrality with respect to the possibility of a person's existing again. The notion appears to be as accommodating on this score as the scriptural notion of the sleep of death is concerning whether that sleep is everlasting (Jer. 51:39) or instead ends in resurrection (Dan. 12:2). Thus if one does not question the claim that a person's death and dissolution entails that he ceases to exist (and, as we have seen, there is reason not to question it), one finds reason to doubt the claim that a person's ceasing to exist entails that he cannot exist again. The notion of a person's ceasing to exist appears to entail nothing of the sort. That notion appears to be neutral with respect to the possibility of afterlife and therefore to accommodate a full range of beliefs and attitudes concerning it.

Let us now turn to the first entailment mentioned above, namely, that a person's death and dissolution entails that he ceases to exist. What reasons are there to doubt that it holds if we suppose (contrary to the evidence just adduced) that the second entailment holds? We can take a short way here by relying on the foregoing discussion of the second entailment. If we suppose it true that a person's ceasing to exist entails that he cannot exist again, then the notion of his ceasing to exist lacks the neutrality just claimed for it. The notion of a person's ceasing to exist that appears in the second entailment cannot, if that entailment is supposed correct, be the neutral notion, but instead one that really does imply that a person cannot exist again. Now if equivocation is to be avoided, this same non-neutral notion must appear in the first entailment, so that it reads as follows: a person's death and dissolution entails that he ceases to exist forever. But, again, there is solid linguistic evidence against this. And it is the same evidence adduced earlier to cast doubt on the second entailment: the same lines of poetry, together with the same reasons for thinking their cease-to-be phrases neutral. Thus if the second entailment is held to be correct and if there is held to be no equivocation on "ceases to exist" in the two entailments, then there are good reasons to doubt that the first entailment is correct. There are, in other words, good reasons for thinking that a person's death and dissolution do not entail that he ceases to exist forever.

This completes our disjunctive criticism of the principle together with its so-called proper application to the case of a person. The principle and its application were stated this way: (a) When a person suffers death and dissolution he ceases to exist; (b) whatever has ceased to exist cannot exist again. Our criticism of this statement is, in sum, that the considerations favoring the truth of (a) render (b) doubtful, and, on the other hand, if (b) is held to be true (a) is doubtful.

Being so eminently dubitable, the principle together with its so-called proper application can no more be used to justify the intuition that people are not gap inclusive than can the principle by itself. (As we saw earlier, since the principle by itself can accommodate intermission-inclusive performances, it can also accommodate one-gap-inclusive people.)

There is a third argument, however, that seems a stronger candidate for this office, an argument contained in or suggested by the following passage from P. T. Geach's *God and the Soul.*[3] I have altered Geach's argument in one particular; I have replaced "material" by "bodily" in the phrase "material continuity," thereby improving the argument's chance of justifying our intuition about gap inclusiveness.

"Let us . . . consider our normal criteria of personal identity. When we say an old man is the same person as the baby born seventy years before, we believe that the old man has [bodily] continuity with the baby. Of course this is not a criterion in the sense of being what we judge identity by; for the old man will not have been watched for seventy years continuously, even by rota! But something we regarded as disproving the [bodily] continuity (e.g., absence of a birthmark, different fingerprints) would disprove personal identity." The important claim in the passage quoted is that bodily continuity is a necessary condition of (or is "required for") personal identity. Two simple cases will illustrate the point. If the police suspect Jones of robbing the grocery store, it can be conclusively proved that Jones is not the (same) person who robbed it by showing that Jones died and was buried six months, say, before the robbery took place. Showing that Jones died six months before the occurrence of the robbery is, in the argument's terms of art, to disprove the robber's bodily continuity with Jones and thereby to prove that Jones was not the person who robbed the store. Bodily continuity and hence personal identity would be disproved, in another such case, if instead of showing that the suspect died before the robbery, we showed that he was elsewhere at the time it took place.

If bodily continuity, then, is a criterion, a necessary condition, of personal identity (as these two cases appear to illustrate), then we have ample support for the intuition that people are not gap inclusive. For to think that they are one-gap inclusive would be to presuppose something false: that bodily continuity is *not* required for personal identity. Moreover, we may reflect that our two cases not only illustrate the claim of the argument, but also epitomize a common and accepted practice, our use of the expression "same person" and its relevant associates. And if we consider this, we will undoubtedly allow that the intuition springs from and reflects that common, accepted practice. Thus the intuition that people are not gap inclusive seems so well supported as to be unassailable. Not only is it the yield of a philosophically unassailable common practice, it is a crop certified indubitable by philosophy itself.

But now we must ask whether the argument adapted from Geach really does justify the intuition. The supposed justification begins in the argument's claim that bodily continuity is a criterion of, is required for, personal identity. What, however, justifies this claim? The argument yields or suggests an answer to this question which we may feel is obviously correct and decisive. I present it in the remainder of this paragraph. Any judgment of personal identity ("Jones is the man who robbed the grocery," "That baby—in the photograph—is Greta Garbo," "Saw Howard Hughes the other day") is false if bodily continuity is not present in the relevant way. And if anyone were to persist in such a judgment on learning or coming to believe that bodily continuity was not present ("Well, even though Jones did die six months before, etc., he *is* the man who, etc.,""What if the baby did die of smallpox long ago? She nevertheless *is* Greta Garbo," "That story about Hughes being at home in the Bahamas when I saw him in Mexico City may well be so—still it *was* Hughes I saw"), he would be justly deemed a fool, a madman, or an oddish philosopher. In sum, the fact that any such judgment is false if bodily continuity is absent is what justifies the claim that bodily continuity is required for personal identity; and that to persist in that judgment on learning of the absence would be laughably queer only emphasizes the undeniability of the justification.

We now have before us a justificatory chain. It presents a claim which, if true, justifies the intuition that people are not gap inclusive. It also presents an alleged fact which, if actual, justifies the claim that justifies the intuition. The reasoning involved is this: We know that people are not gap inclusive, because we know that bodily continuity is required for personal identity; and we know that bodily continuity is required for personal identity by the fact that any judgment of personal identity is false if bodily continuity is not in the relevant way present.

This piece of reasoning stands or falls with the alleged fact just mentioned. If it is not true that all judgments of personal identity are false if bodily continuity is not present, then the claim that bodily continuity is required for personal identity is left unjustified. If, then, there are some judgments of personal identity, a subclass of them, let's say, the truth of which is maintained despite the acknowledged absence of bodily continuity, then it would of course be futile, because question-begging, to attempt to show that they *are* false simply by claiming that bodily continuity is required for personal identity. It is the alleged justification of precisely this claim that would here be in dispute. And if its justification is in dispute, the claim itself remains in doubt. It is doubtful that a doubtful claim can settle any dispute. It is certain that a doubtful claim cannot settle a dispute about its own justification. To think that it can is to think that a claim can be part of its own justification—and to think this is to commit the fallacy of *petitio principii*.

The important point, however, concerning the piece of reasoning under examination is this: If an argument is arrayed against a position that calls the argument's first premise into doubt, then one should recall when examining it that no argument, however sound, justifies its own first premise. Recalling this prompts one clearly to see that an argument so arrayed—as is the one presently under examination—is of no legitimate use. It can be no more than a statement of a counterposition—masquerading perhaps as its own justification.

We have examined an adaptation of Geach's argument. This argument purported to justify the intuition that people are not gap inclusive. If successful, it would show that the theologian's claim that people are one-gap inclusive is false. The first premise of the argument—that all judgments of personal identity are false if bodily continuity is absent—is disputed by the theologian's claim or by what is implied by it, namely, that not all judgments of personal identity made in the absence of bodily continuity are false. If what I have said in the last paragraph about arguments being useless against positions that dispute their first premise is correct, then our argument is of no avail against the theologian's claim, for that claim disputes its first premise. It goes without saying that the argument also does not justify the intuition that people are not gap inclusive.

Our fourth attempt to justify the intuition that people are not gap inclusive begins by assuming that people *are* one-gap inclusive. If then they are one-gap inclusive, of course an alleged resurrectee is the same person as one who died. Identity seems to be justifiably asserted here. What, however, does it mean to say that an alleged resurrectee and someone who has died are the *same* person? Look at the case. What we have is a human being "arising" who looks and acts like someone deceased, whose putative memories fit the life of the deceased person, and who sincerely claims to be that person. But what does it mean to say that he *is* that person? It can mean no more than the features of the case allow. And we have just seen what they are. So to say that he is that person who died is to say something that means no more than that he looks and acts like him, has putative memories that fit his life, and sincerely claims to be him. But if this is all that the assertion of identity can come to here, then it comes to no more than the assertion of exact similarity: it comes to no more than saying that the human being who has "arisen" is a second person indistinguishable from the person who died. To assert identity where this assertion means more than exact similarity requires that there be a feature or features present that distinguishes the case from one of exact similarity. But *per hypothesis* the present case contains no such distinguishing feature or features. Thus though one can *say* that the alleged resurrectee is the same person as someone who has died, one's assertion of identity collapses into one of exact similarity—for it is only the latter that the features of the case allow. But if the assertion of identity collapses into one of exact similarity, then the assumption that people are one-gap inclusive cannot be floated. For the thought that the *same* person lives again after a gap of death can *mean* no more—because the features of the case allow no more—than that there arises sometime after the death of a person another exactly like him. Thus, we justify the intuition that people are not gap inclusive by showing that the thought that they are (one-) gap inclusive does not and cannot mean what it says, that it can come to no more than what the features of the case allow: an assertion of exact similarity.

This argument is a *reductio ad absurdum*. It would justify the intuition that people are not gap inclusive by first assuming true the opposite of this, that is, by assuming that people are (one-) gap inclusive—and then showing that this can mean no more than that after they die people will be succeeded by their duplicates, thereby reducing the purported opposite to absurdity. Briefly, the scheme of the argument is this: of course people are not gap inclusive, for the opposite of this (as the argument shows) is literally unthinkable.

But the argument is broken-backed. Despite indications to the contrary, it does not take seriously its assumption that people are (one-) gap inclusive, for the premise mentioning the features that determine the meaning of the identity assertion omits to mention the feature of gap inclusiveness. If one assumes for the sake of argument that people are (one-) gap inclusive, then one is assuming gap inclusiveness to be a feature of people—as it is a feature of some movies to include an intermission. If, then, one seeks to determine the meaning of the identity assertion in question and concludes that it can come to no more than an assertion of exact similarity, this conclusion shows not that the original assumption (that people are one-gap inclusive) is false or literally unthinkable, but rather that it has been forsaken, quietly dropped in midargument. It is as though one set out to demonstrate that the action following the intermission in a dramatic offering was a second play rather than the second act of a single play and in the course of his demonstration ignored an obvious and admitted feature of the proceedings that clearly doomed his enterprise from the outset: the dramatic offering is a one-intermission-inclusive play. Thus the intended reduction to absurdity of the assumption that people are (one-) gap inclusive does not succeed. And the argument fails to justify the intuition that people are not gap inclusive.

Let us make a fifth attempt to justify this intuition. Like the fourth attempt, it begins by assuming the opposite of what it would prove. (It owes a heavy debt to Bernard Williams's Guy Fawkes argument. For a presentation and discussion of this argument, see Chapter 1.) The attempt goes this way: Suppose that people are (one-) gap inclusive. Then surely an alleged resurrectee—that is, a "risen" human being who looks and behaves like someone deceased, whose putative memories fit the life of the deceased person, and who sincerely claims to be that person—is identical with, and not merely exactly like, the deceased person. But *can* an alleged resurrectee be identical with (rather than a mere duplicate of) a deceased person? Consider. If one such "resurrectee" can be imagined to arise to claim to be Mr. A, who died, then two can. In such a case, to identify both "resurrectees" with Mr. A would be absurd, for it would follow from this identification that the two "resurrectees" are the same person, Mr. A, and also that Mr. A is in two places at once. These absurdities can be avoided by identifying only *one* of the "resurrectees" with Mr. A. It is vacuous, however, to identify either "resurrectee" with Mr. A. There are no grounds for a preference. The grounds present justify only the judgment that either is, or both are, exactly similar to Mr. A. Now respecting a judgment of identity as against one of exact similarity, the grounds in this case involving two pretenders are *the very same* as in the case involving only one pretender. Therefore, in the case involving one, the grounds present justify only a judgment of exact similarity, not one of identity. And if one insists that in this case the "resurrectee" is identical with Mr. A, this can come to no more than that the "resurrectee" is exactly similar to Mr. A.

But if the grounds present do not justify a judgment of identity, then no alleged resurrectee, no person appearing after the so-called gap, can be Mr. A. That is to say, no supposed "second installment" of Mr. A can be *Mr.* A in any part of his history or life, but at best can be only a likeness, a double, a simulacrum of Mr. A. And this implies that Mr. A is not and cannot be (one-) gap inclusive. Thus what we began by assuming true is shown to be impossible; and the intuition that people are not gap inclusive is justified.

Like the argument preceding it, this one too has the form of a *reductio*. It would justify the intuition that people are not gap inclusive by first assuming that people *are* (one-) gap inclusive and then showing that the grounds present do not allow the judgment of identity that this assumption requires, that they allow at best only a judgment of exact similarity.

But also like the argument that precedes it, this one is unsuccessful. It fails to show that the grounds present do not allow the judgment of identity required by the assumption that people are (one-) gap inclusive.

The argument's flaw is in its supposition that the lesson of the case involving two pretenders applies to the case involving one pretender. The lesson does not, in fact, apply. Let us agree that the grounds present in the case involving two pretenders render a judgment of identity vacuous.[4] Let us also agree that the grounds or features are the same in the case involving one pretender. It does not follow that these grounds render a judgment of identity vacuous in the latter case.

Consider an argument that is logically analogous to the one under consideration. (1) If amoeba A has undergone mitosis and become a pair of identical twins, amoeba B and amoeba C, to identify one of the new amoebas rather than the other one with amoeba A would clearly be vacuous, since there would be no grounds for a preference: *both* B *and* C are spatio-temporally continuous with A. (2) Therefore if amoeba A does *not* undergo mitosis, to identify amoeba A at 3:15 P.M. with amoeba A five minutes earlier would also be vacuous since the grounds in this case are the *very same* as in the mitosis case: that is, spatio-temporal continuity.

This argument's conclusion, (2), is obviously false. The spatio-temporal continuity of A (at 3:15) with A (at 3:10), so far from rendering a judgment of identity vacuous, is (in *this* case) sufficient for identity. Consider a laboratory worker, who for the past five minutes has been keeping a constant eye on one amoeba in a field of them magnified and projected onto an overhead screen. He can answer a newly arrived colleague's question "Is *this* one 'our' amoeba?" affirmatively or negatively with perfect certainty because he knows (and, if asked, can tell) that the one his colleague is pointing to is either continuous or not continuous with the amoeba chosen five minutes earlier for his constant surveillance.

And though the argument's conclusion, (2), is obviously false, its premise, (1), is just as obviously true: the spatio-temporal continuity of both identical twins with amoeba A renders a judgment of the identity of either of them with amoeba A vacuous.

Clearly, then, the vacuity of an identity judgment in the mitosis case does not imply that an identity judgment in the nonmitosis case is also vacuous. Or, to put the point more generally, the fact of two equally well qualified pretenders rendering an identity judgment vacuous does not entail the vacuity of an identity judgment where there is but one pretender. Even though there is vacuity in the two-pretenders case, there may yet be none in the one-pretender case. And this is so whether the pretenders are amoebas or men.

Between the amoeba argument and the argument about human beings there is a disanalogy that may seem to render the amoeba argument ineligible for the role I have given it. The disanalogy is this. Whereas in the amoeba argument's premise the vacuity-making feature is that both identical twin amoebas are *continuous* with amoeba A, in the human argument's premise the vacuity-making feature is that both identical twin "resurrectees" are *discontinuous* with Mr. A. This difference, however, does not matter. What matters is that continuity in the one and discontinuity in the other premise are *both vacuity-making features*. Just as both new amoebas' continuity with amoeba A renders vacuous a judgment identifying one of them with A, so also both "resurrectees'" discontinuity with Mr. A renders vacuous a judgment identifying one of *them* with Mr. A. It is this similarity between the premises of the two arguments that allows us to see that vacuity in neither one-pretender case is entailed. For if the fact that discontinuity produces vacuousness in the two-"resurrectees" case entails vacuity in the one-"resurrectee" case as well, then, likewise, the fact that continuity produces vacuousness in the mitosis case entails vacuity in the nonmitosis case; and we see that since the latter entailment cannot be admitted, the former entailment must be denied.

Another point to be made about the argument under consideration concerns its deceptiveness. The argument would divert our attention from what is important in the two-pretenders case. The lesson of that case is that where there is *more* than one (equally well qualified) pretender, a judgment of identity is vacuous. Stating it in this way makes it clear that the lesson does not apply to a case in which there is only one pretender. The argument diverts our attention, however, by making it seem that what is important is the uniformity of features—that what matters is that just as the two pretenders look and act like Mr. A, make sincere memory claims fitting Mr. A's life, and sincerely claim to be Mr. A, so the lone pretender does also. We are led to think that since the features of the one pretender are the same as those of the two pretenders, he stands no better chance of being Mr. A than either of them does. The vacuity actually enters, however, with the multiplication of pretenders, for it is just where there is more than one (equally well qualified) pretender that the one-one condition necessary to the identity of individual substances is absent.

The argument under consideration fails, then, to show that what it calls the "grounds" renders vacuous the judgment of identity required by the assumption that people are (one-) gap inclusive. The argument fails to show, in other words, that this its initial assumption is false or impossible—and so fails to justify the intuition that people are not gap inclusive.

We have now examined five attempts to justify the intuition that people are not gap inclusive: Flew's "one beginning" argument, the argument suggested by van Inwagen, an argument adapted from one by Geach, and two attempted *reductios*. We have seen that all five fail. We must not conclude from this, of course, that the intuition *cannot* be justified. Nevertheless, I submit that we now have reason to *suspect* that it cannot.

III

But now let us remove to a more moderate and perhaps more readily justifiable position: not one that claims that people are not gap inclusive and hence that an alleged resurrectee must be an exactly similar second person, but instead one that holds that the case's features do not *compel* us to hold that the alleged resurrectee is some pre-mortem person rather than a second person exactly like him. This is the position taken by Terence Penelhum in chapter 9 of his book *Survival and Disembodied Existence*, and I rely on his lucid presentation of it:

> At some (unspecified) future date, a large number of persons will appear, in bodies like (or somewhat like) our own here and now. Each one will claim to be some person long since dead, will have putative memories that "fit" his claim to be that person, and will physically resemble that person. It is clear that there is no difficulty about conceiving the sort of existence such people would have; in particular, since they would have human bodies, there is no difficulty at all about their being persisting, re-identifiable individuals *in this future state*. The problem is whether or not they are identifiable with us, the pre-mortem beings who died. It

> seems to me that there is no compelling reason for saying that they cannot be; nor is there any compelling reason for saying that they have to be.

Penelhum goes on to show why he thinks there is no compelling reason either way. It is, he says, because there is a time-gap "between the death of the one body and the appearance of the resurrection-body" that all necessity disappears for identifying an alleged resurrectee as some pre-mortem person. On the other hand,

> certainly the time-gap does not necessitate a refusal to identify in this case . . . there is no need for persons to be regarded as necessarily continuous entities; they might exist like television serials do, in instalments. . . . We can, reasonably, decide for identity, but we do not have to. And this seems to leave the description of the future life in a state of chronic ambiguity. One could only *tell* an imaginary objector that his scepticism was mistaken, since it is hard to give sense to the apparently stronger move of informing him that he would discover that he personally would appear as one of the inhabitants of the resurrection world. In order to have grounds for telling him that he cannot reasonably decide his way [that is, for exact similarity] one would once again need, at least, the ability to use the independently intelligible notion of bodiless personality. And the [picture] seem[s] designed to make no use of it. . . . [Thus] a matter of great cosmic moment seems to hinge on a linguistic decision, . . . [for] the grounds seem ineluctably incomplete.

I believe Penelhum's view to be vulnerable to two criticisms. The first, developed under A below, strikes at his conclusion; it allows, for the sake of argument, that there is an (apparent) ambiguity in the description of the resurrection case at the place where Penelhum claims to find one, but contends that the ambiguity is removable. The second criticism, developed under B below, strikes at Penelhum's premise; it does not allow, even for the sake of argument, that the description of the resurrection case is ambiguous and seeks to show that Penelhum provides no real reason to think it (even removably) ambiguous.

A. Allowing, for the sake of argument, that the resurrection case is ambiguous, we can say that Penelhum's position is comparable to that of one who has just finished closely inspecting the painted portrait of a man and rightly finds it to be ambiguous: the subject may be Robert Frost or it may be George C. Marshall. He finds it reasonable to say that it is Frost, but he finds it as reasonable to say that it is Marshall. He finds that if he were to "identify" the subject as Frost rather than as Marshall he would merely be making "a linguistic decision," that he could only *tell* a "skeptic" who "identifies" the subject as Marshall that he is mistaken, for he sees that the portrait, being perfectly ambiguous, yields no grounds for telling the skeptic "that he cannot reasonably decide his way."

Now it should be clear that although this person may be quite right in thinking that the portrait is ambiguous in the way described and hence that it yields no grounds for telling the skeptic that his position is not reasonable, it would be quite wrong of him to conclude that he could only tell the skeptic that he is mistaken. For although the portrait may be quite ambiguous, the grounds need not for that reason be "ineluctably incomplete" for saying that the subject is Frost (say) rather than Marshall. The ambiguity of the portrait does not leave its description "in a state of chronic ambiguity." A remark of Wittgenstein's (in *The Blue and Brown Books*, p. 32) suggests why. He says, "An obvious, and correct, answer to the question 'What makes a portrait the portrait of so-and-so?' is that it is the *intention*." This reminds us that although a portrait may be ambiguous in the way described, there nevertheless may be complete or decisive grounds for affirming that it is (say) Frost's and for denying that it is Marshall's—these grounds consisting in the consideration that the painter *intended* it to be Frost's.

Just as it would be a mistake to hold that the grounds must be ineluctably incomplete for saying that the portrait is one (say) of Frost rather than of Marshall, so also it is a mistake to hold that the grounds must be ineluctably incomplete for saying that the alleged resurrectee is (say) Smith, a pre-mortem person who died, rather than a second person just like him. For just as the ambiguous portrait case allows the use of something more than just the (neutrally conceived) characteristics of the painting to determine its subject's identity, so the resurrection case allows the use of something more than the (neutrally conceived) characteristics of the alleged resurrectee to determine his identity. We say that in the case of the portrait this something more is the painter's intention to "do" Frost, not Marshall. The something more in the resurrection case is God's *intention* to raise us, not the likes of us. I wish to emphasize here that I am only pointing out a feature of the doctrine of resurrection that I take Penelhum to have overlooked—a feature the overlooking of which has led him wrongly to hold that "the description of the future life [is] in a state of chronic ambiguity." I take my point to be one that can be acknowledged by theist and atheist alike, for our discussion concerns only the coherence, not the truth, of the doctrine.

I will now present and respond to two objections to my use of the notion of God's intention. The first objector allows that cases like that of the ambiguous portrait might be settled by reference to the painter's intention, but he denies that the resurrection case can similarly be settled by reference to God's intention. He presents his case for this by means of a parable.

"Once there was a master potter. He made not only the most durable and serviceable pots in the land, but also the most beautiful ones. Moreover, his work was most various. He made soup pots, flower pots, watering pots, coffee pots, stew pots, tea pots, chamber pots, poker pots (for the fireplace); pots shaped like birds, lions, books, dice, men; pots with snouts, lips, ears, feet, handles; graceful pots, tall pots, cluttered pots, clean pots, lean pots, squat pots. The potter was so accomplished that there was no plan, no conception, that he could not swiftly bring to superb realization. But the potter grew proud. One morning he said to himself, 'Today I will create a pot of simple elegance, but it will be the most unusual pot ever made. Today I will create a pot with an intermission! It will be my finest creation!' And he set to work. Some time later he gazed admiringly at the simple and elegant pot in his hand. He studied it closely to memorize its every detail. Then he smashed it on the floor. He swept up the pieces, threw them in the trash, waited fifteen minutes and then readied a new batch of clay. Some time later, for the second time that day, the potter gazed admiringly at the simple and elegant pot in his hand. He signed, 'Ah, now it's finished. I have created the world's only pot with an intermission; the only gap-inclusive pot ever! I knew I could do it!'

"First," says the objector, "to describe what the potter does as creating a pot with an intermission is plain nonsense. Second, saying that the potter *intended* to create a pot with an intermission plainly does not save that description from being nonsense. What he does do is to make a pot, smash it, and then make another pot like it. Similarly, in the resurrection case, to describe what God purportedly does by saying that he creates gap-inclusive people or that he will raise *us* (not our doubles) on the Last Day is absurd; and saying that according to doctrine God *intends* to create gap-inclusive people or to raise us does not save *that* description from absurdity. What God can be said to do is to create people, allow them to fall to dust, and then create other people who are their doubles."

In response to this objection, two points need to be made. First, for someone holding Penelhum's view the question of whether God's intention does or does not save the description from absurdity cannot arise. To raise this question is to abandon Penelhum's view. For according to this view the description, so far from being absurd, is *reasonable*—as reasonable as: "He will raise up our doubles." What is not thought absurd cannot be thought capable or incapable of being saved from absurdity. The second point is this. If the above objection is made by someone who, unlike Penelhum, holds that the description in question is not reasonable, then he must *show* that it is not, and no mere analogy with pots, no mere parable, accomplishes this. Earlier we considered five arguments that it might be supposed could be marshaled for this purpose. But we have already seen that they fail to justify the intuition that people are not gap inclusive. It seems clear enough that they would also fail to justify our parabolist's charge of absurdity against the description "God creates gap-inclusive people" or the description "God will raise us on the Last Day."

I will now present and respond to a second objection to my use of the notion of God's intention. This objection, unlike the first one, can be made by someone holding Penelhum's view, and it is directed against the portrait case as well as the resurrection case in that it questions the idea that intention can be introduced to resolve the sort of ambiguity the two cases exemplify. Specifically, the objection is this. It cannot be said unambiguously that either God or the artist has fulfilled his intention, for what each produces contains no feature that distinguishes it from something that does not or would not fulfill it: from our doubles, in the resurrection case; from a portrait of Marshall, in the artist case. It can only be said that it is *reasonable* to hold that each has fulfilled his intention; but it must also be recognized that it is *equally* reasonable to hold that he has *not* fulfilled his intention. The question whether he has fulfilled his intention can be answered yes unambiguously only if what he produces to fulfill it yields decisive grounds for its unambiguous identification. But we have already seen by Penelhum's argument that the grounds are ineluctably incomplete. And we now see that, since the intention cannot be said unambiguously to be fulfilled unless those grounds are complete, it is merely question-begging to introduce the notion of intention to resolve the ambiguity. For since the grounds for identifying what is produced are ineluctably incomplete, the grounds for saying that the intention has been fulfilled are also ineluctably incomplete, and so the intention cannot be looked to to complete the grounds for identification.

Whether this objection defeats my claim to have found in God's intention grounds to complete those that Penelhum finds ineluctably incomplete depends on the truth or falsity of its opening claim, that it cannot be said unambiguously that either God or the artist has fulfilled his intention. Since the objection comprehends the artist case and since that case seems more readily understandable, I will examine the objection mainly in terms of it. Why now, according to the objection, can it not be said unambiguously that the artist has fulfilled his intention to "do" Frost? The answer given is that the portrait contains no feature that distinguishes it as Frost's rather than Marshall's and consequently one can hold only that it is reasonable (and undecisive) to say that the artist has done Frost while recognizing that it is equally reasonable (and undecisive) to say that he has done Marshall. But *would* it be equally reasonable in this case either to say that the artist has done Frost or to say that he has done Marshall?

Imagine the following scene. You are visiting the studio of Andrew Wyeth. Looking at a freshly painted portrait standing on an easel, you say to Wyeth, "That could only be either Robert Frost or George C. Marshall." He looks at his work with a fresh eye. After a moment he replies, "You know, you are right. I hadn't even thought of Marshall, though. No; it is Robert Frost."

Where the question concerning the identity of the man in the portrait arises just from the fact that the portrait contains no feature distinguishing it as Frost's, and not, for instance, from a concern that Wyeth may be mistaken about the identity of his model, Wyeth's declaration settles the matter. (Wittgenstein's *Blue Book* remark, quoted above, that "the intention" "makes a portrait the portrait of so-and-so" certainly goes too far; nevertheless knowing the artist's intention eliminates the question that arises from the portrait's ambiguity—the ambiguity that is the analogue of the purported chronic ambiguity of the resurrection case.)

Before Wyeth declares himself, and while you are still ignorant of his intention, it is equally reasonable for you to say "Marshall" or to say "Frost." After Wyeth declares himself, however, this is not so. Your being able in this case to say that Wyeth has done Frost and not Marshall—to say unambiguously that he has fulfilled his intention—does not depend on your discerning, independently of Wyeth's intention, that the portrait is of Frost rather than of Marshall. Rather, the revelation of his intention to have done Frost makes it possible for you to say that it is Frost, not Marshall, he has done. It would be clearly absurd of you now to insist that since it is equally reasonable to hold that he has done Marshall his intention cannot unambiguously be said to have been fulfilled—for it is plain that it is false that it is equally reasonable to hold that he has done Marshall. Of course the portrait looks like one of Marshall and so could reasonably be taken for one of Marshall. But however reasonable, it would nevertheless be a mistake to do so. And it would be reasonable to do so only in one who is ignorant of Wyeth's intention.

We have now seen that it is false in the Wyeth case that it is equally reasonable to hold that Wyeth has done Marshall. This is tantamount to seeing that the pivotal claim in the objection under discussion is false. That claim is that it cannot be said unambiguously that either God or the artist fulfills his intention. This claim is based on the supposition that in order to say unambiguously—and here I revert to the resurrection case—that God would fulfill his intention to raise us, it must be possible to discern, independently of his intention, that it is we ourselves who are to be raised and not our doubles and that since it is impossible to do this, God's intention to raise us cannot be said unambiguously to be fulfilled. Our examination of the Wyeth example, however, gives us good reason to doubt that one must be able to discern, independently of God's intention to raise us, that it is we who are to be raised and not our doubles. The objection under discussion fails, then, to provide a reason to deny that God's intention resolves the ambiguity in the resurrection case, as Wyeth's intention resolves it in the portrait case.

B. The foregoing criticism of Penelhum's view strikes at its conclusion. The criticism was this: if the description of the resurrection case is, as Penelhum holds, ambiguous, then it is ambiguous as my portrait case is ambiguous, and the ambiguity is removed by adverting to the notion of God's scripturally announced intention to raise us. In a nutshell this criticism says: *if* there is an ambiguity, it is removable.

The following criticism of Penelhum's view strikes as its premise. It will seek to show that Penelhum provides no good reason to deem the description of the resurrection case (even removably) ambiguous. I will begin with a quotation from his *Survival and Disembodied Existence*, page 102:

> While it seems altogether reasonable, and is certainly logically possible, to *call* the resurrectee the pre-mortem person, and to expect to *treat* him as the pre-mortem person, is this quite enough, when it is not mandatory to do these things . . . to warrant each one of us expecting *himself to be* one of these post-mortem beings in the future?

As the foregoing passage indicates, Penelhum holds that although we can reasonably call the resurrectee the pre-mortem person and can reasonably expect to treat him as the pre-mortem person, there is no warrant for us to expect to *be* resurrectees. Penelhum makes quite clear what in his opinion this warrant would have to be: it would have to be "something carrying the identity of the person" through the time-gap between death and resurrection. Specifically, it would have to be the continuity of the person's body. But because the resurrection doctrine under discussion makes no use of that notion, there is no warrant, in Penelhum's view, to expect to be a resurrectee, there is nothing to make identification mandatory. "[W]ithout the continuity of the body, the identification does not *have* to be performed" (p. 97).

Why does Penelhum think that bodily continuity (or bodily identity) is required for mandatory identification in the resurrection case? The answer to this may seem already to have been suggested: without bodily identity, identifying the "resurrectee" as the pre-mortem person is indistinguishable from merely reasonably treating the "resurrectee" as the pre-mortem person and calling him the pre-mortem person. Penelhum's view does indeed contain or imply this answer to our question, and we shall consider it in due course.

His text indicates, however, that his own primary or basic answer or argument is a different one. (Why I call it primary or basic will become clear later.) It is conventionalist rather than consequentialist. It does not turn our attention to the conflation that would (allegedly) result from doing without bodily identity. Instead, it refers us to "the conventions we now follow in our talk of flesh-and-blood persons" (p. 58).

Why, then, does Penelhum think that bodily continuity or identity is required for mandatory identification in the resurrection case? His answer is to be found in two chapters that precede his discussion of the resurrection, chapters 5 and 7. My formulation of it follows.

Bodily continuity or identity is required for mandatory identification in the resurrection case because in any and all cases "bodily identity is a necessary . . . condition for the identity of persons" (p. 67): We know that bodily identity is required in the one case because we know that it is required in all. What authorizes the claim that it is required in all cases? Convention: "the conventions we now follow," "the conventions that we have." What conventions? It is "a conventional truth ['a truism'] that a person is, whatever else we hold him to be, a continuous physical organism" (p. 59). Since, then, persons are continuous physical organisms, bodily continuity or identity is a necessary condition for the identity of persons—that is, for *mandatory* identification. However, in *some* cases where bodily continuity is absent—cases like those of the resurrection, of Locke's prince and cobbler, and of Bridey Murphy—identification, though not mandatory, is reasonable. What this means for the case of the resurrection is that though one cannot expect to *be* a resurrectee (p. 102), it would be reasonable to expect to *treat* each "resurrectee" *as* some pre-mortem person and to *call* him that pre-mortem person (p. 102).

As the foregoing answer or argument indicates, I take Penelhum's ultimate premise to be what he calls a truism: that a person is, whatever else we may hold him to be, a continuous physical organism. It is, I believe, this so-called truism that must be seen, in Penelhum's thought, as the first link in a justificatory chain leading to the view that bodily continuity or identity is *required* for mandatory identification in the resurrection case, and hence to the view that there is no warrant for us to expect to be resurrectees.

But as in our discussion of the argument adapted from Geach (the third argument in section II, above), so here too we must observe that a chain of justification is of no avail against positions that dispute or contradict its first link. And surely those theologians who hold the position that Penelhum's chain would reduce to ambiguity will wish to point out that their own position contradicts that chain's first link. For though they will allow, and indeed insist, that Penelhum's truism holds for non-eschatological matters, they will deny that its application extends to eschatological matters. They will say, "Of course a person is a continuous physical organism. But this 'conventional truth,' as you call it, embraces only non-eschatological conventions. Or call it a plain matter of fact: it is a fact about this world, not about the world to come." Thus will the Althaus-Heim theologian deny the applicability of Penelhum's truism to last things, holding instead that a person's continuity is interrupted just once, that he is just one-gap inclusive, the gap occurring between his death and his resurrection.[5]

Penelhum's truism does not justify its own application to last things. Nor does the justificatory chain in which it is a link justify that application; for being its first link, the truism is the (supposed) justifier, not the justified. Thus neither the chain nor the truism is of any avail against the view that a person is one-gap inclusive.

What must be stressed, however, is the following. Penelhum's argument leaves unjustified the truism's application to last things. Thus, the application to last things of the *second* link in Penelhum's argument is left unjustified—the second link being this: "Bodily continuity or identity is a necessary condition for the identity of persons." At best Penelhum's argument justifies only for *noneschatological* cases the notion that bodily continuity is necessary for personal identity. His argument therefore gives us no reason to think that bodily continuity or identity is *required* for mandatory identification in the resurrection case, and hence no reason to think that there is no warrant for us to expect *to be* resurrectees.

To summarize our results so far in section B: We have asked why Penelhum thinks that bodily continuity or identity is *required* for mandatory identification in the resurrection case. We have seen that the truism or conventional truth that a person is (at least) a continuous physical organism yields no satisfactory answer, that it fails to justify the view in question.

But besides this conventionalist response to our question, Penelhum's text also suggests the consequentialist answer we have already noticed. It is this. If there is no bodily continuity or identity carrying the identity of the person through the time-gap between death and resurrection, then identifying the "resurrectee" as the pre-mortem person is indistinguishable from merely reasonably treating the "resurrectee" as the pre-mortem person and calling the "resurrectee" the pre-mortem person. Thus for *mandatory* identification (and warrant for expecting to *be* a resurrectee) bodily identity is required. And so, though Penelhum's conventionalist argument fails, his consequentialist argument seems to succeed.

To repeat, the latter argument is that identification of resurrectee as pre-mortem person is not mandatory, for nothing carries the identity from the death of the pre-mortem person to the appearance of the resurrectee; there is a time-gap. But here we must think of the view according to which a person is a one-gap-inclusive creature, comparable to a one-intermission-inclusive play. Reminded of this view, we realize that it is only if one has overlooked or rejected it that one can think that unless the time-gap is bridged by "something carrying the identity of the person" identification will not be mandatory. Only if a person is *not* gap inclusive, only if he is not like the play, will the mandatory identification of resurrectee and pre-mortem person require a gap-bridging, identity-carrying something. For if a person *is*, like the play, one-gap inclusive, then to think that such a something is required is absurd—as absurd as thinking that for the act following the intermission to be unquestionably part of the *same* play as the act preceding the intermission, an intermission-filling something (an additional act or scene) is required.

Thus we see that Penelhum's consequentialist argument succeeds only if a person is not a gap-inclusive creature. The question, then, is this: is he or isn't he? And now it should be clear why, earlier, we characterized Penelhum's conventionalist argument as primary or basic. For it is evident that it is that argument that would, if successful, justify the negative answer to this question. Briefly, the argument says that bodily continuity is required for mandatory identification; for bodily continuity is a necessary condition for personal identity, because it is a conventional truth or truism that a person is, whatever else we hold him to be, a *continuous* physical organism. But, as we have already seen, the argument's last-mentioned and basic premise is contradicted by the one-gap-inclusion view that the argument would undermine, and this renders the argument useless against that view. The conventionalist argument fails to show that a person is not gap-inclusive. And because of this failure, the consequentialist argument fails to demonstrate that for mandatory identification bodily identity or continuity is required. For only if a person is not a (one-) gap-inclusive creature, is it true that there is such a requirement.

I have tried in the present section, section B, to show that Penelhum has no good reason for saying that the description of the resurrection case is ambiguous, for saying, that is, that a description in terms of exact similarity and one in terms of identity are equally well (and equally ill) justified. In calling the description of it ambiguous, he is claiming in part that it would be reasonable to expect to treat the resurrectee as the pre-mortem person and to call him the pre-mortem person. In claiming that this would be reasonable, Penelhum means that it would be *merely* reasonable; it would not be mandatory—identification of resurrectee as pre-mortem person would not be mandatory. But he has failed to show that it would not be mandatory. (Neither of the two arguments that bear on this point—the conventionalist argument and the consequentialist—succeeds, as we have just seen.) Thus he has failed to show that it would be *merely* reasonable and so has not justified the claim of ambiguity, for, again, part of that claim is that it is reasonable, merely reasonable, to expect to treat the resurrectee as the pre-mortem person and to call him the pre-mortem person.

We have now examined Penelhum's position and found it vulnerable to two criticisms. First, we have seen that if the description of the resurrection case is ambiguous, as Penelhum claims, then it is ambiguous as the portrait in my portrait case is ambiguous and so its ambiguity is eliminable by adverting to the notion of God's intention, so that it would be absurd to think it reasonable to say of Penelhum's "large number of persons" whose rising is understood to be in fulfillment of God's intention to raise *us*, that they are our doubles. Second, we have seen that Penelhum provides no good reason for thinking that there is an ambiguity. Such a reason would have to be one that shows that persons are not (one-) gap-inclusive creatures. Neither the conventionalist and consequentialist arguments extracted from Penelhum's text nor the five arguments examined earlier (Flew's "one-beginning" argument, the argument suggested by van Inwagen, the "bodily continuity" argument adapted from Geach, and the two *reductios*) succeed in showing this.

IV

Before turning to a consideration of a quite different skeptical position, I will examine one more argument that may support the view that persons cannot be (one-) gap-inclusive creatures. Suppose that Smith has been resurrected and then a year later another arises who claims and believes that he is Smith. What would the appearance of this new Smith do to our judgment concerning the first Smith? What retroactive effect would that appearance have on that judgment? After the second Smith appeared, would we not have to say that our earlier judgment was vacuous? For would not the second Smith have equal right with the first to be identified as Smith?

It seems to me that there would be the same degree of temptation (or justification), no more and no less, to renounce our earlier judgment of identity as there would be to renounce yesterday's judgments of identity of each other if tomorrow there arose duplicates of us. In neither case, it seems to me, would earlier judgments of identity be deemed vacuous for the later appearance of duplicates.

"Ah, but the cases are crucially different! In the non-eschatological case the new arrival is obviously not in contention, for he is not spatio-temporally continuous with the original, whereas the earlier pretender, of course, is. But in the eschatological case neither pretender is spatio-temporally continuous with the original. So in the non-eschatological case there is no contest: the pretender who is spatio-temporally continuous with the original *is* the original. In the eschatological case, however, there is a contest between the pretenders—and the contest ends in a tie."

This objection is ill conceived. The two cases are, to be sure, different, but there is no reason to think them crucially different. For although spatio-temporal continuity is present and apparently decisive in the non-eschatological case, and not present at all in the eschatological case, something equally clearly decisive is present in the eschatological case. What appears to settle the identity-exact similarity question in the latter case is that the earlier pretender will have appeared on the Day. Faced with this question, we can say that those who appear on the Day of Resurrection and Judgment (if that Day come) are those whose appearance fulfills the promise of resurrection (I daresay the Day itself, should it come, will be unmistakable); whereas pretenders whom we imagine to appear later could no more be the dead raised than tomorrow's duplicates of us could be us. Thus in neither case does it appear that a later duplication would disturb an earlier judgment of identity.

Of course appearance on the Day would not serve in *every* imaginable case to distinguish resurrectee and duplicate, and I have introduced that factor here only to cope with the objection just presented. A case in which this factor could not serve would be, for example, one in which two pretenders appeared simultaneously on the Day. Appearance on the Day is, of course, no help *here*, in distinguishing resurrectee and duplicate, for both pretenders alike appear on the Day.[6]

Lest it be concluded, however, that the usefulness of this factor is rendered everywhere questionable by its uselessness in certain imaginary cases, consider that spatio-temporal continuity is also useless in some cases. If our best friend undergoes "mitosis" before our astonished eyes, the factor of spatio-temporal continuity is not going to help us decide which of the resulting pair is our friend, for both are spatio-temporally continuous with him. If the factor of appearance on the Day is rendered everywhere questionable by its uselessness in the case of two pretenders appearing simultaneously on the Day, then so is the factor of spatio-temporal continuity by the case of our best friend undergoing "mitosis."

Something important emerges here. It may well be true that the notion that people are one-gap inclusive would in a manner be defeated by the realization of certain imaginable situations—such as one in which, for every person who has died, two or more pretenders appear on the Day. Reflecting on this, one may think that unless a notion is free of such defeasibility it must be somehow incoherent or not viable and so convince oneself that the notion that people are one-gap inclusive has to be given up. But to require for its coherence or viability that a notion be free of such defeasibility is absurd. The presence of this defeasibility is not a symptom of incoherence or lack of viability; moreover, if it were, the notion that people are *not* gap inclusive, that they are continuous entities, would also be incoherent. And, I suppose, no one, least of all our skeptic, would agree that this is so. Again, if it is true that the notion that people are one-gap inclusive is defeasible by certain situations, then it is also true that the notion that they are not gap inclusive is so defeasible—for instance, by a situation in which all of us undergo "mitosis." And if this defeasibility were symptomatic of incoherence in the former, then so it would also be in the latter notion. Both notions might well sink in imaginary high seas, but this gives us no reason to think them unseaworthy in real and normal waters.

V

At this point in our discussion the dialectic "conditions" are such that they precipitate a new rain of skepticism, and the new differs most significantly from the old. Unlike his cousins, our new skeptic allows that those who appear on the Day (if that Day come) may very well be resurrectees. For him resurrection is a genuine possibility. The target of his skepticism is not ontic; it is epistemic. He insists that though the Day may see actual resurrectees, knowledge that they are resurrectees could never be attained. The particulars of his position will emerge in what follows.

Our new skeptic enters the discussion. "I am sorry, but I have disturbing doubts about some of your remarks of a moment ago. Concerning what you called the factor of appearance on the Day, you said that in some cases it will be of no help in distinguishing resurrectee and duplicate. Your example was one in which two pretenders appear simultaneously on the Day. Of course you are right; appearance on the Day is no help here. Nor will I contest your claim that appearance on the Day is as useful in distinguishing resurrectee and duplicate in the case in which one pretender appears on the Day and a second pretender appears a year later, as spatio-temporal continuity is in distinguishing you from your duplicate who appears tomorrow.

"The trouble, however, with appearance on the Day is that it is no help in *the* case. I mean that case in which *no* duplications are imagined. This is the case of resurrection as faithfully and simply drawn as it can be. It is the case in which only one pretender for each person who has died appears on the Day of

Judgment and no other pretenders appear either before or after the Day. There are, to use your words, no imaginary high seas, only real and normal waters. This is the case in which appearance on the Day is of no help. And help is assuredly needed. For although no second pretender is imagined to appear, still we have the *notion* of a simulacrum, that is, of a 'person' who to all appearances is some (other) person, even seeming to have that person's past. And this is all that is required to raise a doubt. Having merely the notion of a simulacrum, we must wonder what it is that guarantees that the pretender who arises on the Day is not a simulacrum instead of the person who died—for it is surely possible that the pretender be a simulacrum. The case seems comparable to this. A rich man dies, leaving his fortune to a son Reggie, who has long been away. A lawyer claiming to represent the son promises to produce him at the reading of the will. The lawyer arrives with his client on the appointed day. Everyone is satisfied that the client is Reggie until someone remembers that the heir to the fortune has an identical twin brother, Tom. Mightn't the client be Tom, whom the father had despised, instead of the real heir? Certainly the fact that the client arrived at the appointed hour does not guarantee that he is the heir, that he is not the despised brother. Now whatever the difficulties in determining the identity of the client (and they might, of course, be insuperable), they pale beside those in the resurrection case. For whereas an investigation into the identity of the client would at least have point (though might fail), an investigation into the identity of the alleged resurrectee to determine whether he is the resurrectee or a simulacrum would not even have point. It could not succeed, for by hypothesis the most thorough of investigations would turn up the same data whether the pretender is the resurrectee or is only his simulacrum."

Here one may wish to respond to our skeptic in the following way. "If by hypothesis the most thorough investigation would turn up the same data in either case and would therefore be pointless to undertake, then by the same hypothesis there *is* no distinction between resurrectee and simulacrum. And so to ask what guarantees that the pretender who arises on the Day is not a simulacrum instead of the resurrectee is to pose a mistaken question. Where there is by hypothesis no distinction between resurrectee and simulacrum, there can and need be nothing guaranteeing that the pretender who arises on the Day is not a simulacrum. For 'resurrectee' and 'simulacrum' will simply be two words expressing a single concept.[7] The situation is comparable, then, to one in which Reggie, the heir to his father's estate, appears at the appointed hour for the reading of the will and it turns out that he not only has no twin brother but himself bears the name Tom as well as his more familiar name Reggie. If one thought that the heir had a twin brother Tom and did not know that the heir was himself called Tom as well as Reggie, then one might understandably demand to know what guarantees that the client is not Tom. But once one's misunderstanding of the matter is eliminated, one can no longer understandably make such a demand. Just so in the resurrection case. Once one understands that there is no difference between resurrectee and simulacrum and so also understands that 'resurrectee' and 'simulacrum' express the same concept, one will no longer demand a guarantee that the pretender is not a simulacrum instead of the resurrectee. For 'simulacrum' is, as it were, just another name for 'resurrectee,' rather as 'Tom' is merely another name for Reggie."

This response to the skeptic is unsatisfactory on two counts. (1) Let us accept for the moment the argument that because an investigation could not show the pretender to be the resurrectee rather than a simulacrum there is no distinction between resurrectee and simulacrum and so "resurrectee" and "simulacrum" express the same concept. To say that these two words express the same concept does not tell us what concept it is. The response is therefore tendentious in making it appear that the concept expressed is that of personal identity rather than that of duplication.

And the response certainly does have this bias. One place the bias is evident is in the response's concluding sentence: "For 'simulacrum' is, as it were, just another name for 'resurrectee,' rather as 'Tom' is merely another name for Reggie"—as though a pretender is really a resurrectee but may by courtesy be referred to as a simulacrum. The bias, for all the argument shows, is perfectly reversible, so that the concept expressed is made to appear to be that of duplication rather than that of personal identity. The response's concluding sentence would then read: "For 'resurrectee' is, as it were, just another name for 'simulacrum,' rather as 'Reggie' is merely another name for Tom"—as though a pretender is really a simulacrum, though may by courtesy be referred to as a resurrectee.

(2) The second count on which the response to the skeptic is unsatisfactory is that its argument, left unexamined in the foregoing paragraph, is unconvincing, and will be especially so to the skeptic. He demands to know what guarantees that the pretender is not a simulacrum rather than the actual resurrectee. And he will insist that the argument in the response to him fails to show that a resurrectee and a simulacrum are not distinct and his demand therefore pointless. He will say, "The fact that investigation cannot show a pretender to be a resurrectee rather than a simulacrum does not entail that being a simulacrum and being a resurrectee are the same thing. And in fact they are not the same thing. If a pretender is a resurrectee, then his past includes an 'earthly' life; if he is a simulacrum, his past does not include an 'earthly' life. This is enough to show that although it is impossible to know whether a pretender is a resurrectee or a simulacrum, being the one is different from being the other."

Let us be quite clear about our new skeptic's position. He holds that the pretender either is the resurrectee or is a mere simulacrum of the person who died and that to be the one is not to be the other, since to be a resurrectee is, among other things, to have a certain past and to be a simulacrum is, among other things, to lack that past. Thus the skeptic allows that ontologically there are two quite distinct possibilities and that if the so-called Day of Resurrection does dawn, one or the other of these possibilities will be realized. But though the pretender must be either the person who died or a simulacrum of that person and though to be the one is not to be the other, the skeptic holds that it is impossible to know which the pretender is, so that even if the pretender is the person who died it is impossible to know that he is not a mere simulacrum. It is impossible to know because the data any investigation could provide would be the same in either case. Thus the skeptic holds that what is ontologically two is epistemologically one. So, convinced that his question cannot be answered, he asks what guarantees that the pretender is not a simulacrum rather than the person who has died.

It should be clear that our skeptic's position is different from Penelhum's and from Flew's. (1) It differs from Penelhum's in that, whereas our skeptic holds that to be a resurrectee is not to be a simulacrum but that it will be impossible to know which the pretender is, Penelhum holds that the resurrection situation is chronically ambiguous. He does not mean that one is in a state of irremovable ignorance concerning the pretender's identity. One knows full well what is the case and therefore understands that it is not a matter of the pretender's being (ontologically) either a resurrectee or a simulacrum. One understands, rather, that it is a matter of the pretender's identity being *ontologically* perfectly "ambiguous," with the result that what is left to one is a coin-tossing decision whether to say that he is the resurrectee or to say that he is a simulacrum.[8] (2) Our skeptic's position differs from Flew's in that, whereas our skeptic holds that the pretender may be the person who died (though if he is, that he is cannot be known), Flew holds that the pretender cannot be the person who died and so must be only his simulacrum.

To deal properly with our epistemological skeptic it is important to be clear about what, in his difference from his cousins, he must concede. He must concede that death and dissolution constitute no bar whatever to the pretender's being numerically identical with the pre-mortem person. For our skeptic it can be no objection to this identity to observe that pre-mortem persons suffer that fate—just as it can be no objection to a stage presentation's all being the same play to observe that the presentation is interrupted by an intermission. This concession is actually required by our skeptic's position, for without it he could not claim merely that we must forever remain ignorant of the pretender's identity.

It is against the background of this concession that our skeptic makes his argument, which can be put as follows. "Suppose the resurrection does occur—suppose that it *has* occurred. We, the resurrectees, can never know that it has, because we can never *know* that we are the same persons who lived the pre-mortem life. We can never know this because (a) we have the notion of our own simulacra and (b) the data any investigation can provide must be the same whether we are resurrectees or simulacra: the same memories (or 'memories'); the same appearance; the same character, personality, abilities, likes, desires; the same innocent conviction that we lived an earthly life, died, and now live again."

The doubt that this argument engenders should not trouble us resurrectees. It is virtually unintelligible. He who in his resurrected life would harbor it must in this present life be prepared to doubt his own identity on rising each morning. He must be willing to say, by parity of reasoning, that since he has the notion of his own simulacrum, he himself may be a mere simulacrum of the person who went to sleep in "his" bed last night and that if he is a simulacrum he is undetectably so even to himself. He must also be prepared to doubt everyone else's identity for the same kinds of reasons.

Our argument here is the precise analogue of our skeptic's. Cast like his, ours goes as follows. "It cannot be known that I am the person who slept unobserved in 'my' bed last night because (c) we have the notion of that person's simulacrum and (d) the data that any morning-after investigation can provide must be the same whether I am that person or his simulacrum: the same memories (or 'memories'); the same character, etc., etc."

Surely we will not be brought by considerations (c) and (d) to doubt that I am RTH, who retired and slept unobserved in RTH's bed last night. Likewise, in the resurrection life, surely we will not be brought by considerations (a) and (b) above to doubt that we are the pre-mortem persons who died. Or, at any rate, if we are brought to doubt in the resurrection case, we must allow that our doubt is the same thin, Cartesian doubt that is possible in the morning-after case; and if we ignore or scorn it in the latter case, we must do so in the former.

Against the temptations of epistemological skepticism these ad hominem reflections are, I believe, good proof. If further consideration seems to suggest that they are not, I submit that without one's quite realizing it one's epistemological skepticism is turning itself into another sort: fortunately it is the ontological sort we have already considered at length and found wanting.

VI

Noticing that all the arguments we have examined are unsuccessful, we are in position to summarize our examination of Flew's, Penelhum's and our skeptic's objections to the doctrine of resurrection as follows. (1) Flew argues that the resurrected Flew could only be "an imitation of the Flew that had been destroyed" in death and dissolution. But justification of this claim requires that it be shown that people are not (one-) gap-inclusive creatures, and no argument we have examined—certainly not Flew's own—shows this. (2) Penelhum argues more moderately that the description of the resurrection case is chronically ambiguous, that identification of the resurrected Flew as the Flew who died is not mandatory. But justification of this claim too requires showing what no argument examined shows: that people are not (one-) gap inclusive. (3) Our epistemological skeptic argues that the alleged resurrectee may indeed be Flew, but it cannot be known that he is. We have just seen how this objection dies of embarrassment. All three objections to the doctrine of resurrection founder. Their supporting arguments give neither the believer nor anyone else reason finally to be perplexed by such words as these from the Babylonian *Talmud:*

> On seeing Israelitish graves, one should say: Blessed is He who fashioned you in judgment, who fed you in judgment and maintained you in judgment, and in judgment gathered you in, and who will one day raise you up again in judgment. . . . He will one day revive you and establish you. Blessed is He who revives the dead;

and by such words as these from *The Authorised Daily Prayer Book of the United Hebrew Congregations of the British Empire:*

> In the abundance of his lovingkindness, God will quicken the dead. . . . May his great name be magnified and sanctified in the world that is to be created anew, where he will quicken the dead, and raise them up unto life eternal.

Of course, there may be other arguments that would succeed in justifying a perplexity about the identity of resurrectees. I suspect, however, that there are not. Moreover, I suggest that anyone who is perplexed without having or being able to propound a justifying argument is perplexed not because he has caught a glimpse of something logically amiss in those eschatological uses, but perhaps because of their novelty to him and because of a common philosopher's incapacity to read or hear some pieces of language without unwittingly imposing alien requirements on them. If this suspicion and this suggestion are correct, one who does not allow his acquaintance with these eschatological uses to dissolve his perplexity is hardened indeed by philosophy, and if he continues to find the notion that people are one-gap inclusive "wildly counterintuitive," it appears that his intuition is just the parochial product of a one-sided diet.

As a postscript I wish to make one or two comments concerning possible paraphilosophical sources of resistance in this issue. To do so I will set forth an objection to the use I have made of analogies to plays and stories, and then I will respond to the objection. The objector says: "The theologian's and your repeated use of analogies to plays with an intermission and to stories presented in two installments gives rise to a suspicion. The suspicion is that the theologian and you do not really grasp the significance, the momentousness, of death. An intermission in the performance of a play is not an annihilation of something, not a ceasing to be. But the death of a man is his annihilation. Death is, in the pithy vulgarism of our time, *it*. One suspects in these theologians a failure of imagination. But perhaps not a simple failure. Perhaps it is a willful failure, motivated by the same fears and desires that social commentators see in our society's shunting aside or disguising the grimness and pain of death. One suspects, to put it bluntly, that the repeated use of the story and play analogies is the philosophical twin of the California drive-in mortuary.

"But speculation about motivation aside, I cannot escape the feeling that there is a failure of imagination, and that if the theologian did grasp death's significance he would no longer have any heart for disputing the skeptic, for he would no longer have any inclination to think of death as like a play's intermission. The poets stand willing here to assist the flagging imagination. Writing of his dead Lucy, Wordsworth gives us this powerful quatrain:

> No motion has she now, no force;
> She neither hears nor sees;
> Rolled round in earth's diurnal course,
> With rocks, and stones, and trees.

Lucy's death an intermission? Assuredly not! In death she has returned to nature, to dust; she has *become* rocks and stones and trees!

"And for a black-comic version of the same message I know of none better than this from *Hamlet:*

> *King:* Now, Hamlet, where's Polonius?
> *Haml:* At supper.
> *King:* At supper! Where?
> *Haml:* Not where he eats, but where he is eaten. A certain convocation of politic worms are e'en at him. Your worm is your only emperor for diet. We fat all creatures else to fat us, and we fat ourselves for maggots. Your fat king and your lean beggar is but variable service, two dishes, but to one table. That's the end.
> *King:* Alas, alas!
> *Haml:* A man may fish with the worm that hath eat of a king, and eat of the fish that hath fed of that worm.
> *King:* What dost thou mean by this?
> *Haml:* Nothing but to show you how a king may go a progress through the guts of a beggar.

Like the fat king and the lean beggar, we are in death all of us dishes at one table. We are all food for worms. And, as Hamlet says, that's the end. The *end*—not 'the intermission'!"

Perhaps this is enough to enable a feeble imagination to grasp the grievous, monstrous significance of death. What is not noticed by the objector, however, is that his own imagination may be failing—failing to grasp the significance (the dreadful, as well as the awesomely glorious significance) of the doctrine of the resurrection. Kierkegaard contemplated the failure to grasp the dreadful aspect of the doctrine in these acidly ironic words: "Once upon a time people tried to escape the thought of eternal punishment in thoughtlessness and defiance,—now . . . the whole educated world bears witness that it is nonsense, and one makes oneself ridiculous by entertaining such ideas" (*Journal*, X^2

A552). Kierkegaard's remark also suggests a motivation for the possible failure of the objector's imagination. If the dread of death dampens the theologian's imagination, leading him to employ "inappropriate" analogies, perhaps the dread of judgment dampens the objector's (and "the whole educated world's") imagination, leading to employment of "inappropriate" analogies, for example, the reduction to dust of a stick of chalk or the destruction of a pot. Tit for tat.

But if paraphilosophical considerations can help at all to explain the sources of this eschatological issue, perhaps dread and a dampened imagination are the terms of a relatively shallow diagnosis. Perhaps the sources are better explained in terms of the belief-formed life and the unbelief-formed life. Obviously such lives can breed opposed attitudes toward imminent death. It is reported that a month before his death, that firm and energetic unbeliever Mark Twain wrote to a friend gruffly rejecting an attempt to comfort him in his last days: "Isn't this life enough for you? Do you wish to continue the foolishness somewhere else? Damnation, you depress me!" Two months before his death, an equally firm and energetic believer, C. S. Lewis, wrote this marvelous letter to a friend:

> What a pleasant change to get a letter which does *not* say the conventional things! I was unexpectedly revived from a long coma, and perhaps the almost continuous prayers of my friends did it—but it wd. have been a luxuriously easy passage, and one almost regrets having the door shut in one's face. Ought one to honour Lazarus rather than Stephen as a protomartyr? To be brought back and have all one's dying to do again was rather hard.
>
> When you die, and if "prison visiting" is allowed, come down and look me up in Purgatory.
>
> It *is* all rather fun—solemn fun—isn't it?[9]

The certainty concerning last things that these letters exhibit clearly goes deep in both men. And all I wish to suggest is that, where the parties to a philosophical discussion of last things remain in a way unmoved even after all their objections and replies have been made, where they still feel that they don't really understand each other even though each now finds the other's position philosophically unobjectionable, what may remain ineradicably to keep them apart is the marrow-deep conviction that is manifested (and fed) by the way of one's life.

Notes

Introduction

1. "Nominalism," *Sophia*, 3 (July 1962), 6.
2. *Death and Immortality* (London: Macmillan, St. Martin's, 1970), p. 49.

1. Puzzle Cases and Earthquakes

1. I put quotation marks around the name "Erik" in order not to seem to be closing the door, at the outset, on the notion that it is correct to call this man Viljanen.

2. B. A. O. Williams, "Bodily Continuity and Personal Identity: A Reply," *Analysis*, 21 (1960), 43. For additional material concerning Williams's argument, see the fifth argument in section II, Chapter 6.

3. *Proceedings of the Aristotelian Society*, 56 (1956–57), 237–241.

4. The likelihood that Williams would say something much like this is substantiated by passages on pages 43 and 48 of his *Analysis* paper.

5. This is not to say that Volter might not on some occasion say such things. He would do so on those occasions when, as he would put it, his father misremembered. If, for instance, the reminiscence concerning the beach were one of these occasions, Volter might say, "No, Father. You didn't take me; it was Uncle Risto—don't you remember?" The reader will have noticed that there are relevant here two sorts of contexts in which Volter speaks of "Erik": one is that in which he responds to people who challenge his reaction to "Erik"; the other, that in which he responds to people who share that reaction and ask such ordinary questions as "Has your father left for rehearsal?" In what follows I

will make no special point of the difference between them. What is important for my purpose is that Volter uses "my father" in both.

6. *Analysis,* 21 (1960), 22–23.

7. This sense of "understand" is not an invention of mine. In the parable of the sower, Matt. 13:18–23, the criterion of a man's understanding the message of the kingdom is that it produce a "good crop" in his life: "The seed sown among thorns represents the man who hears the message, and then the worries of this life and the illusions of wealth choke it to death and so it produces no 'crop' in his life. But the seed sown on good soil is the man who both hears and understands the message. His life shows a good crop, a hundred, sixty or thirty times what was sown."

8. For more concerning this distinction between two sorts of understanding, see the remarks concerning Mark Twain and C. S. Lewis in the postscript to Chapter 6. There it is suggested that even if someone gains "philosophical or intellectual understanding" of the doctrine of the general resurrection, that is, even if he comes to allow that the doctrine is free of what is philosophically objectionable, still it may be that "he sees it all as nonsense" (see following note) or as another of "the fairy tales of religion" (Freud). Or in a humbler mood—a mood (say) of sad self-reflection induced by the thought that some good friend, for whose intellect and character he has great respect, accepts and lives by this doctrine (as well as the others)—he might, like our speaker in the Viljanen case, say, "*I* do not understand. I can't go along." Here he admits that he lacks the condition whose mark is "going along" or "participation"—the "good crop" of the parable of the sower.

This, in the religious case, is the condition that, according to Saint Paul, only "the Spirit" can supply (see following note and section IV of Chapter 2). And if Paul is right, the difference between this "spiritual understanding" and the understanding that philosophical investigation and reflection might bring is so much the clearer, for one is not helpless to achieve the *latter* sort of understanding, whereas the former sort is not achieved, but given.

But even if one rejects the notion that only "the Spirit" can supply spiritual understanding, one may nevertheless feel compelled to acknowledge the spiritual sort as well as the philosophical. As already suggested, an "outsider" like our speaker in the Viljanen case or like the sad, self-reflective unbeliever just sketched may do so. Perhaps even a Freud or a Mark Twain may acknowledge both sorts, though for an atheist rampant doing so would doubtless be more difficult than for an atheist couchant.

9. Cf. 1 Cor. 2:14: "An unspiritual person is one who does not accept anything of the Spirit of God: he sees it all as nonsense; it is beyond his understanding because it can only be understood by means of the Spirit."

2. *Paradox—or Illusion?*

1. There is reason to question my assumption and to suspect, not that no such change in intellectual climate has occurred, but that it occurred, or at least began, much earlier than Pratt believes it did. As early as the 1730's Bishop Butler issued this puzzled complaint:

> It is come, I know not how, to be taken for granted by many persons, that Christianity is not so much as a subject of inquiry; but that it is, now at length, discovered to be fictitious. And accordingly they treat it, as if, in the present age, this were an agreed point among all people of discernment; and nothing remained, but to set it up as a principal subject of mirth and ridicule, as it were by way of reprisals, for having so long interrupted the pleasures of the world.

This passage is from the advertisement (dated May, 1736) to Butler's *Analogy*. I will not examine the question about chronology it raises. My interest, as will shortly be seen, is in another facet of the matter. In any case, perhaps it is a mistake to try to fix a time when a great secularization took place, a time before which the mass of men required transcendental explanations and believed that they could not live without answers to the ultimate questions. Perhaps there was never such a time. A reader of the manuscript reminds me that Jesus taught that many take the road to perdition, only a few the road that leads to life and that Genesis records that even before the Flood the thoughts in the hearts of men, only Noah excepted, "fashioned nothing but wickedness all day long." Such observations, by no means confined to Scripture, suggest that *any* attempt to fix a time (more recent than the Fall) of a great secularization is folly since it is based on the sentimental supposition that there was once a time when most men did believe.

2. Such, for instance, as those suggested by Renford Bambrough on pp. 50–51 of *Reason, Truth and God* (London: Methuen, 1969) and by Alasdair MacIntyre on pp. 176–177 of *Metaphysical Beliefs* (New York: Schocken, 1970). See, also, part one of Huston Smith's "Do Drugs Have Religious Import?" *Journal of Philosophy*, 61 (1964).

3. Compare Freud, "A Religious Experience," *Collected Papers*, vol. 5 (London: Hogarth Press and The Institute of Psycho-Analysis, 1957).

4. Both in Scripture and in later Christian documents. See the following passages in Scripture: Matt. 16:17; John 6:37, 44, and 65; 1 Tim. 1:13–14; 1 Cor. 15:10; Gal. 1:15–16; Eph. 2:8–9 and 6:23; Ezek. 11:19–21; Acts 2:47, 3:26, 11:22, 13:43, 14:27, 15:4, and 21:19. Consider also this passage from Augustine's Epistle ccxvii (to Vitalis).

> 30. . . . If, as I prefer to think in your case, you agree with us in

> supposing that we are doing our duty in praying to God, as our custom is, for them that refuse to believe, that they may be willing to believe, and for those who resist and oppose his law and doctrine that they may believe and follow it. If you agree with us in thinking that we are doing our duty in giving thanks to God, as is our custom, for such people when they have been converted . . . then you are surely bound to admit that the wills of men are *prevented* [started, set going] by the grace of God, and that it is God who makes them to will the good which they refused; for it is God whom we ask so to do, and we know that it is meet and right to give thanks to him for so doing.

In addition, consider that the following proposition was anathematized by the Council of Trent in 1547, fixing Catholic teaching on the point.

> 3. That without the prevenient inspiration of the Holy Spirit and his aid a man can believe, hope and love, or can repent, as he should, so that on him the grace of justification may be conferred.

These two passages are included in *Documents of the Christian Church*, selected and edited by Henry Bettenson, 2d ed. (Oxford: Oxford University Press, 1963), pp. 77–78 and 370.

5. It has been proposed to me that the falsity of the doctrine is not implied by Freud's thesis and that the fact that it is not is shown by the possibility of a believer's accepting Freud's thesis without relinquishing his status as a believer. The proposal is that the believer could allow that belief stems from an unconscious wish but insist that the wish itself has its source in God. (Perhaps one thinks here of the Christian idea of divine discontent.) This attempt at reconciliation, however, deals irresponsibly with Freud's thought. Freud meant to exclude the idea that the wish has its source in God, just as one who asks me to show the children a game means to exclude gaming with dice even though its exclusion does not come before his mind (see Wittgenstein's *Philosophical Investigations*, p. 33.) And that Freud meant to exclude it is clear from his talk of "fatal resemblances" (see below) and from many other details in his book.

6. C. S. Lewis, *God in the Dock* (Grand Rapids, Mich.: Eerdmans, 1970), p. 261.

7. Compare an experience of Simone Weil's, reported in Jacques Cabaud's *Simone Weil: A Fellowship in Love* (New York: Channel Press, 1964), pp. 169–170. When reciting the poems of the English metaphysical poet George Herbert, "Simone was at first conscious only of the aesthetic quality of Herbert's work: 'I used to think that I was merely saying beautiful verse; but though I did not know it, the recitation had the effect of a prayer. And it happened that [in

the autumn of 1938] as I was saying this poem . . . Christ himself came down, and He took me'" (the bracketed phrase is Cabaud's). I am grateful to Peter Winch for calling this passage to my attention.

3. Two of Kierkegaard's Uses of "Paradox"

1. There is this difference in the logic of the two cases: the woman's "objective uncertainty" is due to insufficient evidence, whereas Socrates' is due to his continuing dissatisfaction with the rational proofs for immortality which he offers in the *Phaedo* (at least this seems likeliest to be what Kierkegaard has in mind). Kierkegaard himself, however, is not consistent on this point, for, as a passage I will quote later shows, he connects "objective uncertainty" with *evidence for* and *evidence against*. In any case, these differences are not important for the purpose at hand.

2. Cf. *PS*, p. 173: "The way of objective reflection leads . . . to historical knowledge of different kinds." But see also note 1 above.

3. *PS*, p. 192. Also one *confuses* faith with knowledge; cf. ibid., p. 30.

4. Cf. "The sum of all this is objective uncertainty" as it occurs in the passage quoted above.

5. Cf. James L. Muyskens's "James' Defense of a Believing Attitude in Religion," *Transactions of the Charles S. Peirce Society*, 10 (Winter 1974), esp. 52–53.

6. Cf. *The Interpreter's Dictionary of the Bible*, vol. 2, p. 420, col. a, 1st para.

7. See *The Jerusalem Bible*, 1 Cor. 2:14, fn. h.

8. Another alternative open to the unbeliever is to advance a Freudian account of belief. Since this account is discussed in both Chapters 1 and 2, I omit discussion of it here.

9. *Faith and the Philosophers* (London: Macmillan, 1964), John Hick, ed., p. 9.

10. *Fear and Trembling* (Garden City, N. Y.: Anchor Books, 1954), p. 265.

11. *Training in Christianity* (Princeton: Princeton University Press, 1944), p. 125.

12. Irving Copi, *Introduction to Logic* (New York: Macmillan, 1955), p. 77.

13. Cf. Heb. 11:17–19.

4. The Absolute Paradox: The God-Man

1. "The Christology of Wolfhart Pannenberg," *Religious Studies*, 3 (October 1967), 376.

2. "A Programme for Christology," *Religious Studies*, 3 (April 1968), 516.

3. This and the following parenthetical citations are to *Concluding Unscientific Postscript* (Princeton: Princeton University Press, 1941), D. F. Swenson and W. Lowrie, trs.; and to *Philosophical Fragments* (Princeton: Princeton University Press, 1936), D. F. Swenson, tr.

4. The *New English Dictionary* gives "come into existence, sprung" as the "rather neuter signification" of the sense of "born" relevant here, and gives the following Christian phrases to exemplify this sense: "born of the Virgin Mary," "born in a stable."

5. It appears that orthodoxy would not refuse to accept this way of formulating what is found in the scriptural passages cited in the second reaction on the ground that the phrases "existed" and "did not exist" in the formulation misrepresent the content of the passages. For orthodoxy itself, in the persons of Leo and Cyril, speaks of the Incarnation in like idiom: "continuing to be before time, [the Son] *began to exist* in time" (*The Tome of Leo*, my italics); and the "[Son Jesus Christ] is said to have been born . . . after a woman's flesh, though he *existed* and was begotten from the Father *before all ages*" (Cyril's "Second letter to Nestorius," my italics).

6. "A Programme for Christology," pp. 515–516.

7. Ibid.

8. Cp. *Summa Theologica*, III, xvi, A. 4, especially objection number one and its reply.

9. Seeing that the general form of the charge of self-contradiction against the orthodox claim fails, the critic may choose to make a more modest charge, which runs as follows: "All statements of the form and analysis in question are self-contradictory, except those in which what takes the place of X is an expression signifying something representational—a picture, image, or figure. 'The duck-rabbit' and 'the figure' are such expressions here, whereas 'Christ' and 'Jesus' are not." This less comprehensive charge obviously cannot be met, as the bolder one could, by saying that since the remark about the duck-rabbit in the answer to the riddle is not self-contradictory the argument given to support the charge is unsound. For this more modest charge already excepts all such remarks and confines itself to statements whose subject terms signify something nonrepresentational—such as the orthodox statement about Christ under discussion. (I wish to thank Anthony Kenny for suggesting this less comprehensive charge to me.)

What reply can orthodoxy make to this new charge? I think that the proper reply is this: "This new charge makes an exception of 'representational' statements. But a defense against this charge must await the critic's attempt to justify excepting them; in other words, it must await the critic's attempt to justify this *new* charge, for until such an attempt is made, we have been offered no reason to pay it heed. And if the critic does not deem such justification necessary, then by the same token we too can except without justification any statement we wish to—and of course we would straightway except the Christological statement that is the subject of this discussion."

10. *Religious Language* (New York: Macmillan, 1963) pp. 193–200.

11. Ibid., esp. pp. 194–195.

12. Might contemplation of the duck-rabbit figure also show us that there is some confusion in the thought of Cyril when, contending against Nestorius in his "Second letter to Nestorius," he says that the hypostatic unity is "indescribable and inconceivable"? Again suppose that Nestorius is thinking about the matter in the way described above. And suppose Cyril, thinking at the same general level and so also inclined to resort to the same commonplace objects to illustrate his thoughts to himself (the same one-sided diet), to have replied, "True, one thing cannot be two things, have two natures. Cabbages are just cabbages and cannot be ships also. But nevertheless Christ is but one thing (person) and he has two natures, that is, is two things (God and a man). He is the sole exception. But one can no more describe or conceive how this can be so than one could describe or conceive how a cabbage could be both a cabbage and also a ship, should some unimpeachable authority assure one of this."

But if Cyril had bethought himself of the figure of the duck-rabbit, he could have replied to Nestorius, "Your examples of cabbages and ships show how you are misled. Of course, one thing cannot have two natures or be two things, if what you have in mind by this is shown by your example 'A cabbage cannot be a cabbage and also a ship.' But surely you would allow that one thing can have two natures or be two things when what you have in mind is shown by the figure of the duck-rabbit. For here, one thing, the figure (one disposition of a single segment of line), *is* two things (has two natures), a duck and a rabbit." And supposing Cyril to have replied to Nestorius in this way, we can see that he could not have gone on to say of the hypostatic union that it is indescribable and inconceivable—*if* what led Cyril to characterize it in this way was his having something like a "cabbage-ship" model in the back of his mind.

Here an objector says: "But can the duck-rabbit figure rightly be described as something that 'is two things (has two natures)'? Is it not something that has just *one* nature? Is it not, does it not have only the nature of, a line figure? It seems that this is so and that one is tempted to think that the figure has two natures just because one can *see* it as the figure of a duck's head or as the figure of a rabbit's head. The figure seems to be in the same case as Rorschach blots, which though subjects may see them as any number of things, are, for all that, only patterns of ink on a page. And if this is so then the 'one-sided diet of examples' that you suppose to be behind Cyril's thought that the hypostatic unity is indescribable and inconceivable is really not supplemented or enriched, for the duck-rabbit will be just another single-natured morsel like cabbages. Thus, supposing Cyril's thought to be the result of a one-sided diet, you at any rate have not shown us a way to be rid of it."

My reply to this objection goes as follows. It is certainly so far correct to say that the duck-rabbit figure can be seen as the figure of a duck's head or as that of a rabbit's head. But what must not be ignored is that it can be seen as the one or the other *just because it is a two-aspected figure*. It is the figure of a duck's head, and it is the figure of a rabbit's head—one disposition of a single segment of line ingeniously forming both. Moreover, it is a clever artifice whose aspects one can *notice* or *fail to notice*. For instance, one may see that the figure is that of a duck's head but fail to see that it is also the figure of a rabbit's. Thus the objector provides no reason to deny the therapeutic efficacy of the figure. It is its two-aspectedness that enables us to say that if Cyril arrived by the route we have described at his thought that the hypostatic union is indescribable and inconceivable, his thought is not the indication of a holy mystery, but the symptom of his own philosophical mystification—a condition that is relieved as well as produced by certain diets.

13. It might be thought that one can appeal as well to cases of transformation or metamorphosis. Thus: "There is no more reason to think the Christian claim self-contradictory than to think that this remark about an adult frog is self-contradictory: 'As an adult frog, this creature did not exist before last summer; before that time it existed as a tadpole.'" This attempt, however, might seriously mislead one concerning Christian teaching. For according to that teaching, although the Word *became* flesh, in doing so it did not cease being the Word—whereas, of course, when a tadpole becomes a frog, it ceases to be a tadpole. The cartoon figure will not mislead in this way, for although it becomes a duck, it does not cease being a rabbit. In connection with this it is interesting to consider an engagement described by Bernard Williams in his "Tertullian's Paradox" (*New Essays in Philosophical Theology*, Antony Flew and Alasdair MacIntyre, eds. [New York: Macmillan, 1964] p. 207). The engagement is between Marcion, with whom Williams evidently agrees, and Tertullian. Williams writes: "It will be recalled that Marcion had said that if God had been incarnated, he would have changed; but change involves losing some attributes and gaining others; and God cannot do this. Tertullian briskly replied that what Marcion had said was true of temporal objects, but God is not a temporal object, and that therefore what Marcion said did not apply. But this is to counter one's opponent's move by smashing up the chess-board." We can

certainly agree that Tertullian simply smashed the chess-board. But we can also see how Tertullian should have replied. He should have said, "If you mean by saying that God cannot change that he cannot become other than God, then what you say is correct. God cannot change in such wise that he ceases to be God—as a tadpole changes in such wise that it ceases to be a tadpole. But if you mean that God cannot change while remaining God, then your position is both unscriptural and gratuitously restrictive. Are not God's speaking, his becoming wroth, and so forth instances of change in him? And is not the Incarnation another such instance? You seem to be driven to fly in the face of these and other such instances because your conception of change is fed exclusively by examples like that of the tadpole, examples of transformation or metamorphosis. But if you enrich the diet to include examples like that of the cartoon figure, you will find yourself able to allow that God can change—without ceasing to be God—as the cartoon rabbit changes into a duck-rabbit without ceasing to be a rabbit."

Here, also, belongs a comment on a remark of R. W. Hepburn's in *Christianity and Paradox* (New York: Pegasus, 1968), p. 66. Hepburn says, "If we took *literally* the texts, 'He that hath seen me hath seen the Father,' and 'I and my Father are one,' they would seem to imply that God and Jesus were *identical*. But a little reflection shows that this would be immediately disruptive of several fundamental Christian ideas. For one thing, . . . it would mean that when God became incarnate, he no longer dwelt also in eternity." Reading these texts with the help of the cinematic duck-rabbit, we see that we can take them in a way that does not imply that when God became incarnate, he no longer dwelt in eternity, or, in other words, was no longer eternal; just as we see that it would be wrong to think that when the rabbit figure became a duck-rabbit, it ceased to have the character of a rabbit's head. And it is not obvious that this way of taking the texts would be less literal than the way described as literal by Hepburn. But whether less literal or not, it is, I think, the way (in Augustine's phrase) of "the prudent, careful, and devout reader."

14. That there are difficulties involved here, and abiding ones, may be gathered from a reading of pages 517 through 519 of the C. J. F. Williams article referred to in note 2. (See also *The Historical and Mystical Christ*, A. M. Henry, ed. [Chicago, Ill.: Fides Publishers Association, 1958] pp. 37–38, 45, 63–64, 69, 70.) The problems for orthodoxy there described may be viewed as stemming from orthodoxy's rejection of the thesis that it was a man that the Son assumed. Certainly had orthodoxy accepted this thesis, the problems Williams describes would not have arisen for it. See the following passages of *Summa Theologica* for material concerning this rejection: III, iv, A.A. 2 and 3; ii, A. 6;

and xvi, A.A. 1 and 4. For passages relating to the difficulties to which this rejection leads, see: III, iv, A. 4; ii, A. 2, reply obj. 3, A. 3, reply obj. 2, and A. 5, reply obj. 2; iv, A. 2, reply obj. 1, and A. 4, reply obj. 3.

15. That Aquinas does this is evident not only from his remark that "it cannot properly be said that the Son assumed a man, granted (as it must be, in fact) that in Christ there is but one suppositum [person] . . ." (III, iv, A. 3), but also from his saying "to assume is to *take something to* oneself" (III, iii, A. 1, my italics; see also III, ii, A. 8 and iv, A. 2).

16. Not "in" in the sense illustrated by one's pointing to a "still" version of the duck-rabbit figure and saying, "There is a duck in that figure. See it?" but in the sense illustrated by one's saying of a cupful of water that one has poured into one's bath that it is in one's bath.

5. *Free Will and God's Foreknowledge*

1. *Papers on Time and Tense* (New York: Oxford University Press, 1968), pp. 31f.

2. NO here assumes that if "God's foreknowledge" of the great episode in its infinite scope and infinitesimal detail has a satisfactory sense, then language must contain conceptual materials whereof to construct a model or analogy that displays that sense. (A satisfactory sense here is one that (a) makes God's foreknowledge *worthy* of God and (b) does not make it abrogative of freedom.) OD shares this assumption. It remains unquestioned throughout this paper. My colleague Don Levi has convinced me, however, that it should be explored, though I can do no more here than to indicate the area needing exploration. Why, Levi asks, must it be supposed that if "God's foreknowledge" of the great episode makes satisfactory sense, a model that will display that sense must be constructable? He allows that models can be constructed to meet specific skeptical arguments—as Augustine meets a particular argument of Evodius' to the incompatibility of God's foreknowledge with free will by means of an analogy with *men's* foreknowing each other's actions: Evodius' argument is defeated by this analogy because the argument rests on the presupposition that foreknowledge *per se* is incompatible with freedom and because Evodius allows that men *do* foreknow each other's *free* actions. But apart from such specific defensive uses of models, Levi sees no need for them in this matter.

To employ a figure presented by P. T. Geach in lecture: The Book of the World contains God's knowledge. The pages already turned (his knowledge of the past) and the page at which the Book stands open (his knowledge of the present) are full. Are the pages yet unturned (his knowledge of the future) also full? Levi thinks so and thinks too that he understands this and thinks moreover that no model must be constructable for it to be understandable. But with Geach I am inclined to think that the unturned pages are only partly filled, that there are many blank portions, and that the idea of their being full is unintelligible—unless a model is constructable that will display a satisfactory sense of "God's foreknowledge" of the great episode.

3. See Kenny's "Divine Foreknowledge and Human Freedom" in his *Aquinas* (Garden City, N.Y.: Anchor Books, 1969), pp. 255f. and Prior, "Formalities of Omniscience."

6. The General Resurrection

1. From *The Christian Hope* (Philadelphia: Muhlenberg, 1954). See Althaus's article "Eschatology" in *Handbook of Christian Theology* (Cleveland: Meridian Books, World, 1958), especially pp. 103–104. See also Robert McAfee Brown's two articles, "Immortality" and "Soul (Body)," in the same volume; section 1b of the article on Soul in *The Interpreter's Dictionary of the Bible*, vol. 4; Oscar Cullmann's essay in *Immortality and Resurrection*, Krister Stendahl, ed. (New York: Macmillan, 1965); footnote a to 2 Macc. 7 and footnote c to 2 Cor. 5 in *The Jerusalem Bible*. For my present purposes the important points emerging from the foregoing citations are two. (1) The true Hebraic-Christian notion of man is that he is a psychophysical unity, not "two separate, independent entities," body and soul, the latter notion being a Greek adulteration of true doctrine. (2) According to the unadulterated doctrine, when a man dies he "returns to dust," nothing of him surviving, and on the last day he is raised up to eternal life. Needless to say, these points are points of contention among exegetes. Fortunately, however, my concern is not to determine whether these points are exegetically correct. I will instead *suppose* them to be correct and then try to determine whether the picture they contain of death and resurrection can withstand the scrutiny of the skeptical philosopher.

Another matter to be noticed here is one concerning such language as the following: "Lucy ceased to be." "He is no more." "Thou'lt come no more. Never, never, never, never, never." The finality of death is what is suggested or stressed by these phrases. Now when the Althaus-Heim theologian says that nothing in man is capable of resisting the destructive power of death and that when we die we pass into nothingness, it may seem that he too is stressing the finality of death. It may look as if he is giving his theological endorsement to the feelings of finality expressed by "He is no more" and the like.

He is not doing this, however. He is, instead, setting his face against the dualist picture of afterlife. He is saying that the soul does not survive death, that a man dies in both body and soul (later to be resurrected in body and soul).

It may be that despite the fact that the Althaus-Heim theologian wishes only to insist, against the dualist, on the "thoroughness" of death, in so insisting he embraces willy-nilly the notion of death's finality. If this is so, however, it must be shown. And this chapter may, I think, fairly be described as an examination of several attempts to show it. My own view—to let the cat a little way out of the bag—is that to insist on the "thoroughness" of death does not commit one to the notion of its finality.

2. See *Locke and Berkeley*, C. B. Martin and D. M. Armstrong, eds. (Garden City, N.Y.: Anchor Books, 1968).

3. London: Routledge & Kegan Paul, 1969, p. 26. Having heard a version of this chapter, Geach has asked me to make it clear to the reader that this argument is not one he finally embraces in his paper "Immortality," but only one he tentatively adopts and finally abandons.

4. It is possible that this should not be agreed to, that even though the grounds present are identical in the two pretenders, a judgment identifying one pretender as Mr. A, the deceased person, would *not* be vacuous. This may be true. My interest here, however, is only to show that even if a judgment of identity is (or were) vacuous in the two-pretender case, this would not entail the vacuity of such a judgment in the one-pretender case. In a word, my interest is not in the truth of the premise but only in whether it, be it true or false, entails what the argument under examination claims it does.

5. If the Althaus-Heim theologian is correct in his scriptural exegesis, then there is, coupled with the secular "conventional truth" noticed by Penelhum, a religious-eschatological "conventional truth" about persons or the use of person words. And so, if the theologian is right, Penelhum may be said not just to have failed to show that the application of the "conventional truth" extends to eschatological matters. His failure would be somewhat more serious than this way of putting it suggests. He would have failed to recognize the existence of a, or a part of the, "conventional truth" about persons or the use of person words. And so instead of saying that he has failed to show that the application of the "conventional truth" extends to eschatological matters, one could say that he has made a false claim as to what the (whole) "conventional truth" is. I believe that in saying this I am remaining faithful to Penelhum's use of the phrase "conventional truth." I take it that in saying it is a *conventional* truth that a person is a continuous physical organism, he is not saying it is *true* that a person is a continuous physical organism or, in other words, is not (one-) gap inclusive. In the light of the present discussion, saying this would appear bold indeed—suggesting, I suppose, that Penelhum had received a personal revelation more convincing to him than the scriptural one has adversaries would call to his attention. No; in reading the phrase "conventional truth," surely we are to

emphasize "conventional" rather than "truth." So we can say that Penelhum's claim as to the *conventional* truth is (given the correctness of the theologian's exegesis) false. And we can say this without abandoning our proper philosopher's neutrality in the matter of whether the doctrine of resurrection teaches *truth* rather than falsehood.

An additional point is this: if the Althaus-Heim theologian is correct in his scriptural exegesis, then the (part of the) "conventional truth" about persons or the use of person words that his exegesis calls to our attention is both ancient and alive. That this is so is suggested by the fact (if the theologian is correct) that material embodying this "truth" dates at least from the time of Judas Maccabeus to the present. See 2 Macc. 7 and 12:43f.; Dan. 12:2–3; Isa. 26:19; the passages from the Babylonian *Talmud* and the *Authorised Daily Prayer Book* that appear in section VI of this chapter; and the references cited in note 1 above. For an additional interesting discussion of these matters see *The Christian Doctrine of Immortality* by S. D. F. Salmond (Edinburgh: T. and T. Clark, 1903), especially chapters IV and V of Book Third.

6. I have already argued in section II of this chapter that even if neither pretender in this case is the resurrectee it does not follow that in the case in which only one pretender appears *he* is not the resurrectee.

7. Compare this with Derek Parfit's view concerning what he calls "a secular version of the Resurrection": "I want to say that those two descriptions—'It's going to be me,' and 'It's going to be someone who is merely exactly like me'—don't describe different outcomes, different courses of events, only one of which can happen. They are two ways of describing one and the same course of events" (quoted in *Personal Identity* by Godfrey Vesey [London: Macmillan, 1974], p. 96).

8. At a meeting attended by Penelhum and myself the question arose whether the ambiguity Penelhum claims to find is epistemological or metaphysical. The query was directed to me after I had read a portion of a draft of this chapter to those assembled. I was stumped. I redirected the question to Penelhum. My present recollection is that his droll response was "I was hoping I wouldn't be asked." The question *is* rather a hot potato. Nor is it one that Penelhum's text now seems to me clearly to answer. I am not aware that Penelhum has dealt in print with the issue. I hope, if he has not, that he will sometime do so. In the meantime, I shall not abandon my metaphysical (or ontological) interpretation of him. For either the epistemological or the metaphysical reading yields a skepticism that is compelling; and if Penelhum's skepticism is, as it turns out, epistemological, then it is in effect his position we are here considering.

Incidentally, the best evidence I find in Penelhum for a metaphysical reading is in the last sentence of his resurrection chapter. Being part of his summation of the chapter's achievement, the sentence seems to provide a particularly important clue to correct interpretation. The point Penelhum is making in the sentence is that the data in the resurrection case are not sufficient for the pretender to *be* the pre-mortem person. The point is *not* that the data are insufficient for our *knowing* that he is. I reproduce the sentence with Penelhum's own emphases: "While it seems altogether reasonable, and is certainly logically possible, to *call* the resurrectee the pre-mortem person, and to expect to *treat* him as the pre-mortem person, is this quite enough, when it is not mandatory to do these things (when its being that person does not follow from the data of our stories) to warrant each one of us expecting *himself to be* one of these post-mortem beings in the future?"

9. *Letters of* C. S. *Lewis*, W. H. Lewis, ed. (New York: Harcourt, Brace, & World, 1966), p. 307.

Selected Bibliography

Recent works relevant to individual chapters in this volume, with the chapters to which they are relevant indicated by numbers in parenthesis following each entry:

ADAMS, MARILYN MCCORD. "Is the Existence of God a 'Hard' Fact?" *Philosophical Review*, 76 (1967), 492–503. (5)

ALSTON, WILLIAM. "Psychoanalytic Theory and Theistic Belief." In *Faith and the Philosophers*. John Hick, ed. London: Macmillan, 1964. (2)

CABAUD, JACQUES. *Simone Weil: A Fellowship in Love*. New York: Channel Press, 1964. (1 and 2)

GARELICK, HERBERT M. *The Anti-Christianity of Kierkegaard*. The Hague: Martinus Nijhoff, 1965. (3 and 4)

GEACH, PETER. "Immortality." In *God and the Soul*. London: Routledge & Kegan Paul, 1969. (6)

HICK, JOHN. "Theology and Verification." *Theology Today*, 17 (1960). Reprinted in *The Existence of God*, John Hick, ed. New York: Macmillan, 1964. (6)

HOLT, DENNIS C. "Foreknowledge and the Necessity of the Past." *Canadian Journal of Philosophy*, 6 (1976). (5)

JOHNSON, HOWARD A., AND NIELS THULSTRUP, eds. *A Kierkegaard Critique*. New York: Harper, 1962. (3 and 4)

KENNY, ANTHONY. "Divine Foreknowledge and Human Freedom." In

Aquinas, Anthony Kenny, ed. Garden City, N.Y.: Doubleday, 1969. (5)

LEWIS, C. S. "Cross-Examination." In *God in the Dock*, Walter Hooper, ed. Grand Rapids, Mich.: Eerdmans, 1970. (1 and 2)

———. "On Obstinacy in Belief." In *The World's Last Night*. New York: Harvest, 1960. (1 and 2)

———. *Surprised by Joy*. New York: Harcourt, Brace & World, 1955. (1 and 2)

MACKINNON, D. M., AND ANTONY FLEW. "Death." In *New Essays in Philosophical Theology*, Antony Flew and Alasdair MacIntyre, eds. New York: Macmillan, 1964. (6)

MUYSKENS, JAMES L. "James' Defense of a Believing Attitude in Religion." *Transactions of the Charles S. Peirce Society*, 10 (1974). (1, 2, and 3)

NIELSEN, H. A. "The Nature and Limits of Scientific Truth." In *Methods of Natural Science*. Englewood Cliffs, N.J.: Prentice-Hall, 1967. (2)

PENELHUM, TERENCE. "The Analysis of Faith in St. Thomas Aquinas." *Religious Studies*, 13 (1977). (1, 2, and 3)

———, ed. *Immortality*. Belmont, Calif.: Wadsworth, 1973. (6)

———. *Survival and Disembodied Existence*. New York: Humanities Press, 1970. (6)

PERRY, JOHN, ed. *Personal Identity*. Berkeley and Los Angeles: University of California Press, 1975. (1 and 6)

PHILLIPS, D. Z. *Death and Immortality*. New York: St. Martin's, 1970. (6)

PIKE, NELSON. "Timelessness, Foreknowledge and Free Will." In *God and Timelessness*. New York: Schocken, 1970. (5)

PRICE, H. H. "Faith and Belief." In *Faith and the Philosophers*, John Hick, ed. London: Macmillan, 1964. (1 and 2)

PRIOR, A. N. "The Formalities of Omniscience." In *Papers on Time and Tense*. New York: Oxford University Press, 1968. (5)

RORTY, AMELIE OKSENBERG, ed. *The Identities of Persons*. Berkeley and Los Angeles: University of California Press, 1976. (1 and 6) (This volume contains a remarkably good bibliography of recent work on personal identity.)

SHOEMAKER, SYDNEY. *Self-Knowledge and Self-Identity.* Ithaca, N.Y.: Cornell University Press, 1963. (1 and 6)

VESEY, GODFREY. *Personal Identity.* London: Macmillan, 1974. Paperback ed., Ithaca, N.Y.: Cornell University Press, 1977. (1 and 6) (This volume contains an excellent bibliography of works on personal identity.)

WESTPHAL, MEROLD. "Kierkegaard and the Logic of Insanity," *Religious Studies,* 7 (1971). (3 and 4)

WILLIAMS, C. J. F. "A Programme for Christology." *Religious Studies,* 3 (1968). (4)

Recent works of interest in the philosophy of religion:

GEACH, PETER. *God and the Soul.* London: Routledge & Kegan Paul, 1969.

———. *Providence and Evil.* Cambridge: Cambridge University Press, 1977.

———. *The Virtues.* Cambridge: Cambridge University Press, 1977.

KELLENBERGER, JAMES. *Religious Discovery, Faith, and Knowledge.* Englewood Cliffs, N.J.: Prentice-Hall, 1972.

NIELSEN, KAI. *Contemporary Critiques of Religion.* New York: Herder and Herder, 1971.

PENELHUM, TERENCE. *Problems of Religious Knowledge.* New York: Herder and Herder, 1972.

———. *Religion and Rationality.* New York: Random House, 1971.

PHILLIPS, D. Z. *Faith and Philosophical Enquiry.* New York: Schocken, 1970.

———. *Religion without Explanation.* Oxford: Blackwell, 1977.

PIKE, NELSON. *God and Timelessness.* New York: Schocken, 1970.

RHEES, RUSH. *Without Answers.* London: Routledge & Kegan Paul, 1969.

Index

PARADOX AND IDENTITY
IN THEOLOGY

Designed by G. T. Whipple, Jr.
Composed by The Composing Room of Michigan, Inc.
in 11 point VIP Electra, 3 points leaded,
with display lines in Bookman.
Printed offset by Thomson-Shore, Inc.
on Warren's Number 66 text, 50 pound basis.
Bound by John H. Dekker & Sons, Inc.
in Holliston book cloth
and stamped in All Purpose foil.

Library of Congress Cataloging in Publication Data
(For library cataloging purposes only)

HERBERT, ROBERT T 1928–
Paradox and identity in theology.

Bibliography: p.
Includes index.
1. Philosophical theology. I. Title.
BT55.H47 1979 230'.01 78-20784
ISBN 0-8014-1222-6